THE CROSS AND THE .357 MAGNUM

PHILIP HICKS

Bridge-Logos
Orlando, Florida 32822

Bridge-Logos
Orlando, FL 32822 USA

The Cross and the .357 Magnum
by Philip T. Hicks

Edited by Kim Grage (www.positiveink.net)

Library of Congress Catalog Card Number: 2006939806
International Standard Book Number 978-088270-320-6

Printed in the United States of America.

Scripture cited from the New Testament is from *The Layman's Parallel New Testament*, specifically, the *Amplified New Testament*. Scripture cited from the Old Testament is from the New King James Version of the *Spirit Filled Life Bible*.

G163.316.N.m701.35250

DEDICATION

My parents, Tom and Eleanor Hicks

Years ago, President George Bush, Sr. introduced an awards program called the "Thousand Points of Light" to honor Americans who've gone the extra mile to bless the lives of others. My wonderful dad, Thomas Roy "Buck" Hicks, whom I call "Pop," was once selected for this honor out of the Memphis area. While he jokingly tells others that he's "one of the brightest" lights, I am wholeheartedly confident that he and my precious mother, Eleanor Jean Hicks, are surely bright lights, empowered and motivated by the love of Jesus Christ.

They have endured much pain and embarrassment due to my prodigal living, but thankfully, they have continued to demonstrate the unconditional love, grace, and mercy of a heavenly Father who patiently calls us home to Him. Throughout my days and years of disobedience, it was the faithful, fervent prayers of my parents that not only kept me alive, but most importantly, called upon the precious Holy Spirit to open my heart and orchestrate the circumstances which led to my crying out and being set free to live the overcoming life that I enjoy today!

It is with much love, honor, and respect that I dedicate this book to my dear parents, who sacrificed so much for my brothers and me, and who were faithful to "train us up in the way we should go" so that when we are old, we will walk the narrow way that leads to eternal life!

John, Rich and Jane

When a person makes Jesus both Savior and Lord of his life, he begins an exciting journey that makes the "fun" experiences of life seem so bland and even boring. For when the Creator of our universe comes to live within a person, both his heart and mind are suddenly opened to the most important treasures of life ... people.

As my story reveals, a few months after beginning my journey with Jesus, He brought John Harber into my life, along with his beautiful family—his wife Beth, daughter Jane, and her husband Rich Moore.

I call John Harber my "spiritual dad," not only because he temporarily stood in for my earthly "Pop," who was so far away in Tennessee, but most importantly because John was brought into my life to show me how a Christian should act toward others. John's walk matched his talk, always demonstrating kindness and graciousness, and encouraging both young and old everywhere he went! He was a man who, like Jesus, gave his time, talents, and resources to meet the needs of others.

If anyone ever provided me a modern day example of "the Good Samaritan," it was my beloved spiritual dad, John Harber. And while John and Beth have now graduated to heaven—no more pain and sickness as they rejoice around the throne of Jesus—I will forever be indebted to them, Jane, and Rich for lovingly supporting and encouraging me during my time of "growing pains" as a young child of God.

Phoebe Young

When I think of my precious friend and sister, Phoebe Young, I'm reminded of God's promise to "surround us with angels lest we dash our foot upon a stone." I was but one day old as a Christian when God sent my guardian angel, Phoebe, into my life! From the beginning I knew she was uniquely different—so full of the love and wisdom of Jesus Christ! I later learned her gracious maturity didn't come easy, as she was refined through the fires of divorce, family rebellion, and disappointments at every turn.

But it was in her weakness that she was made strong, while serving as a missionary in Bahrain, smuggling Bibles into China, training young missionaries for YWAM, ministering in prisons and crisis pregnancy centers, assisting hurricane victims despite having to endure her own hardships, and so much more.

When thinking of Phoebe, I recall the Biblical account of a visit by Jesus to the home of Mary and Martha. While Mary "sat in Jesus' presence," Martha was busy preparing food for him and even feeling a little perturbed that Mary was not helping her. And while Martha's motives were respectable and appreciated, our Savior pointed out that "Mary had chosen the better part." Phoebe is the perfect picture of combining the virtues of both Mary and Martha in her life. Because she spends so much time resting in our Lord, she is routinely empowered to minister healing and wholeness to others as she constantly serves.

I am so honored to call her my sister and friend!

Larry Shook

I was blessed with many wonderful chaplains while incarcerated, but I have chosen to honor one in particular, Larry Shook. This past year our precious Lord called Brother Shook home, and I am confident that he is singing "Holy, Holy, Holy" to our Lord around heaven's clock!

And yet, Brother Shook had begun this song years ago while on earth as he demonstrated the power of praise to so many brothers in blue as well as friends and family on the street. His vibrant joy and smile brought warmth to so many, and he enjoyed a well of wisdom that spoke timely words of encouragement everywhere he went.

As this book reveals, I met relatives of Brother Shook who lived in Memphis and were friends of my parents; this made my world so much smaller while knitting my heart even closer to Brother Shook. When I was called to the chapel to learn of my younger brother's death, it wasn't coincidental that Brother Shook was there with a warm embrace and intercessory prayer that surely reached heaven on our behalf!

He was a man who personally experienced sorrow and sickness; hence, he enjoyed a grace to minister to others who walked a similar path.

True preachers don't retire—they are "refired"—and Brother Shook is a great example of this. After retiring as a prison chaplain, he continued to minister at his church and in other arenas. He had a heart for God and for helping people. No doubt when Brother Larry Shook reached heaven, he was personally met and hugged by Lord Jesus, who said, "Well done, my good and faithful servant. You were faithful with a few things; I will make you ruler over many things. Enter into the joy of your Lord."

I am honored to dedicate this book to a brother who poured into my life as well as the lives of so many others.

ACKNOWLEDGEMENTS

I am deeply grateful to the following for their wonderful support and belief in God's calling on my life. These people have encouraged me to reach others with the love of Christ Jesus and contributed immeasurably toward the birth of my first book.

I am so thankful to my precious wife, Patti, and to Kyle, Chelsie, and Cody for being so patient with me, as a husband and dad, and for loving me despite my many flaws. I love them all so very much!

Many thanks to my Oral Roberts University writing instructor, Reverend Jim Ferrier, and his wife, Connie, for their belief in me.

I am so grateful for my brothers, Ken Birks, Tony Borders, John Vaccaro, and Chris Gunderson (past and present board members of A Merry Heart Ministries) for their discernment, wisdom, and encouragement as I pursue visions and goals that God has placed on my heart. I am especially grateful for their patience and willingness to keep me accountable and a good steward of the gifts entrusted to me.

I am indebted to Kim Grage, owner of Positive Ink (www.positiveink.net), for her endless hours of hard work editing and improving our manuscript to help us transform it into a book that will encourage people from all walks. Many thanks to Kim for her diligent attention to detail.

To Lydia Birks for her kind offer to further proofread our work. Thanks also to Lydia for encouraging the Rock of Roseville to support our ministry.

We believed God would supply the funds to self-publish, and, as always, our Father miraculously provided through the following families from the Rock of Roseville. May their obedience to respond to our Father's leading be rewarded many times over as He multiplies back to them—pressed down, shaken together, and running over!

Randy and Kristen Bertrand
Bruce and Anne Cantrell
Jack and Terri Little
John and Sue Miller
Paul and Brenda Rundus

And most importantly, we give thanks to our *wonderful* heavenly Father who is always faithful to exceed His children's expectations! When He guides, He always provides—that He and He alone be glorified. And best of all, to my dear Savior and Lord, Jesus Christ, for willingly laying down His life that we who receive Him may discover new life in Him!

CONTENTS

CHAPTER 1

TWO STEPS BACK

Warm raindrops splashed against my face as we lowered the coarse rope over the roof's edge. From the top of a Fort Lauderdale apartment building, my eyes nervously searched the parking lot five stories below, and I silently prayed I wouldn't spot any security guards coming by on patrol. My partner, Tom, and I were dressed completely in black, blending perfectly with our starless-sky backdrop.

I tried to remain calm, but my mind was doing flip-flops. After snorting much more cocaine than usual that afternoon and evening, I had attempted to come down by toking on a joint of Colombian Gold, a premium form of marijuana. Instead of bringing me down, the stuff just made me paranoid.

"Look down there!" I yelled. "There's a security guard, and he's looking up here!"

"Shhhh, hold it down," whispered Tom. "That's just someone who got out of that car! They'd have to have bionic eyesight to see us."

It was time to descend to the now-darkened apartment three stories below, whose occupants had already departed. Before gaining access to this wealthy gated community, Tom and I had lain in wait in a grassy field adjacent to the complex. With the help of a pair of military binoculars purchased earlier at a local Army Surplus store, we had monitored the movement of the couple who lived in the apartment and watched as the lights went off. They finally walked across the parking lot, entered their car, and drove away. As soon as the patrolling security guard was out of sight we made our move, successfully scaling a chain-link fence that surrounded the complex then crawling to the edge of the parking lot. Using the parked cars for cover, we slowly maneuvered our way to the building, boldly taking the elevator to the fifth floor before climbing a ladder to the roof. Thankfully, no one crossed our path.

Tom had brought along a 40-foot long rope. After tying one end around an air conditioner vent, he slowly lowered the other end over the edge of the roof.

I insisted on being the one to scale the building. I took a deep breath and eased over the edge. "No problem," I thought to myself. "I've seen this done on detective shows many times before."

Perspiration trickled down my face as I fiercely gripped the rope. I had no trouble as I inched past the fifth floor on my way to the third-floor balcony. The relative ease of my progress temporarily erased my fears until I suddenly froze in terror.

My heart raced while my breath stood still.

There before me—less than six short feet away—stood a woman on her fourth-floor balcony, silently smoking a cigarette as she gazed into the night.

For a moment I thought I was hallucinating, and a million thoughts raced through my mind. Was I losing it? How long had she been there? Had she walked out while I was climbing down? How could I have been so blind? What was I going to do?

"Oh, God!" I whispered. "Don't let her see me."

Scenes of my life flashed vividly before me, and I wondered how I could have been so reckless as to have volunteered to participate in this ridiculous escapade.

I had come to Florida to enjoy a fun-filled vacation, intending to return home to Aspen, Colorado, in two weeks. During the three years that I had lived in Aspen, I made friends with a guy named Al Bishop. Whenever Al visited Aspen, he came with lots of cash, and he didn't hesitate to spend it freely. I introduced Al to many people, including Robin Williams, a young comedian from California. Al told me he kept a beachside apartment in Fort Lauderdale, Florida, which was available to me if I ever traveled south.

When I arrived in Florida, I discovered that Tom, another friend of Al's, was using the apartment, and we became short-term roommates. While partying with Tom, I learned that he, too, was 29 years old and that we had much in common. While I was in Florida to party, though, he was here on business—some very risky business—involving a man named John. According to Tom, John had ripped off some $30,000 in a drug deal that had gone sour six months earlier. He had returned to Florida to recover that loss.

"Can you run that by me again?" I excitedly questioned Tom after he told me his story. "So what happened? What did you do?"

"Hold on," replied Tom, "I'm getting there. What do you think I did? I mean... it was *his* apartment and all he had to do was call the cops and report a burglar was in his place! What was I gonna do... call the cops and tell 'em this guy ripped off my drugs? Hell no... I ran out of there, drove to the airport and flew back to Tennessee!"

And now, six months later, Tom had returned to the scene—or should I say, above the scene—as he was now three stories above me while I dangled helplessly on a rope, about to be spotted by the woman who stood six feet away. I was about to freak out!

"Don't turn this way, lady," I half-prayed, half-whispered. "Go back inside, lady!"

What seemed like an eternity later, the woman turned from the rail, pausing first to toss her cigarette butt into the night before going back inside her apartment. By some miracle, she hadn't spotted me.

I then probably set a speed record for rappelling down a building, as I soon found myself safely on the third floor balcony.

I used a small pry bar to pop open the sliding glass door as Tom pulled the rope back up. He then came down the emergency ladder to the third floor stairwell en route to the front door of the apartment, where I waited. After hearing the light tapping on the door, I let him in and we began ransacking the apartment.

Following an intense search, I found a big roll of $20 bills in a suit coat pocket. My find totaled $5,000.

"Wow, I ain't believin' this!" I said to myself. I dashed into the other room. "Tom," I exclaimed, "look at this!"

"This ain't enough!" whispered Tom, as he thumbed through the bills. "Keep looking." We continued our frantic search for additional cash, looking through every drawer and cupboard we could find.

I came across a box of bullets, but otherwise, we came up empty-handed. Tom decided we'd have to wait on John to return home then force him to come up with the remaining $25,000.

That was when my true colors began to surface, and they were all yellow!

While Tom began looking through a hall closet, I went into the kitchen. I couldn't find anything of value in the cupboards, but out of curiosity, I opened the refrigerator.

My eyes lit up when I spotted a bottle of wine. "All right!" I said, as I examined the label. I could tell it was expensive.

Regardless, I figured it was a good way to get some instant courage. I grabbed the corkscrew and worked on opening the bottle. POW! The cork popped out and I jumped, spewing wine all over the cabinet drawers.

Startled by the noise, Tom ran into the kitchen. "What in blazes was that?" he demanded. He took one look at me, shook his head disgustedly, and walked out.

I was soon sitting in the hallway, sipping expensive wine from one of the fancy crystal wine glasses I'd found. The more I drank, the more I had to get up and use the bathroom. Before long, the commode was filled with cigarette butts, floating in the now-yellow water. I was afraid to flush it for fear a neighbor might hear and know someone was there.

"Here," said Tom. My eyes again lit up as he handed me a gun the size of a small cannon. "I found this .357 magnum in the bedside table. You may need it. This dude could be armed," he added.

Well now... I knew I had done a number of things wrong in my life, and playing cat burglar surely wasn't going to win me any stars in the *Saints' Hall of Fame*, but I didn't want any part of killing anyone! I hadn't signed on for that. All he said we'd have to do was go into the apartment and the dough would be there. He didn't say anything about this before.

My stomach turned into a knot! Why had I ever said yes to this crap?

The cold metal of the gun sent chills down my spine! I quickly laid it aside and resumed my drinking while Tom stationed himself beside a bedroom window, watching for John's return.

I heard a noise at the front door. Moments later, it swung open to reveal a giant of a man. John had finally arrived.

As our eyes met, I don't know who was more surprised—but there was no doubt who was more afraid!

Jumping up, I turned to run away, moving toward the small bedroom where Tom was hiding.

As I charged through the door, I collided with Tom, who was coming out at the same time. This all took place in an instant, and it probably resembled an episode of the Three Stooges.

Tom now stood between John and me.

John's female companion stepped into the apartment and screamed. Tom headed toward her while John dashed into the master bedroom. I grabbed the gun and followed John.

He was leaning over his bedside table, no doubt looking for the gun I now held in my shaking hand.

"All right!" I shouted. "Turn around and raise your hands above your head!"

I fully expected him to turn around, raise his hands and give up, just like they do on television. However, he must've forgotten the script as he charged me!

I was momentarily dazed as I watched John knock the gun from my outstretched hand. But I quickly came to my senses and realized there'd be no more compromise. This was for real. It would be him or me. We both reached for the magnum. Unfortunately, I came up on the short end of the deal.

And yet, from somewhere I drew strength I'd never before experienced, and I held my own. I wrestled with this giant of a man over the large gun he now held.

As we grappled, the gun went off. It fired once... twice... and the third shot made contact with my right leg. The bullet shattered my thigh bone, sending me crashing onto the floor.

For some reason, I pretended I was dead. I lay motionless in a pool of blood, frozen in a state of shock. Since the only light came through the doorway of the living room, my attacker didn't know where I'd been hit; he probably thought I was dead.

John stepped to the doorway, and a gun battle began between him and Tom, who was somewhere in the front of the apartment. The fact that Tom even had a gun was still a shock to me!

As the roar of their guns filled the air, I tried to stand, but I fell right back, grimacing in pain as my leg hit the floor.

Realizing I was still alive, John quickly returned to my side, leaned down, placed the magnum to the side of my head, and fired. All I heard were two loud clicks.

"Damn," he muttered, before throwing the empty gun onto the floor. He then ran out.

I later learned he caught two .44 magnum slugs as he ran past Tom. He was hit in the back and in the arm, but strangely, he didn't die. In fact, he kept going.

Tom locked the door and ran to my side, saying "Let's go!"

"I can't go anywhere," I groaned. "I've been hit and I need a doctor... bad! Don't worry, I'm not gonna snitch on you... take off!"

He did. To this day, I don't know how Tom reached the ground uninjured, as he dropped over the balcony. Then again, maybe he was. No matter, because the cops never found him and I never again saw or heard from Tom.

After Tom split, I dragged myself into the bathroom. I pulled myself up to the sink to get a drink. I was in tremendous pain.

I lowered myself back to the floor and began crawling out of the bathroom. As I tried to turn sideways to drag my leg through, I got stuck. "Ah-w-w-w-w-w-w," I groaned.

I tried to maneuver my body through the narrow doorway and my leg got jammed. The pain was unbearable, and now I couldn't move forward or backward.

I remembered something I heard a preacher man say years before. My folks used to make me go to church. I didn't dig the scene, but the ladies were awesome. Anyway, this preacher was describing the devil and how he operates. "Satan paints a real simple picture in his efforts to lead people astray," began Brother Hartman. "Then, when they go for the bait and get pulled under, it's all over!"

Most definitely, at that time in my life, I knew very little about the devil and how he worked. In fact, anything I knew about "the Man Upstairs," good and evil, and all that was purely head knowledge. The words I once heard would come back to me: A mere nine inches separates a person from hell and heaven—that is, enjoying a "heart" relationship with Jesus versus "head" knowledge or mental assent.

Nevertheless, there was some kind of battle going on inside of me, and it was due to much, much more than the drugs I had taken. One side of me was saying, "It's time to leave," while the other side reminded, "You don't want to be called a chicken, do you?"[1]

My thoughts returned to my present situation when I heard voices in the next apartment and a pounding on the wall. Later I learned the entire apartment complex was crawling with cops, one of which was now talking to me through the wall. Of course, he didn't know who I was, if I lived there, or what.

"Is anybody in there? Hello?" said a gruff voice.

"Yes," I screamed, "and I need help!"

"Open the front door!" he demanded.

"I can't!" I yelled. "I've been shot, and I can't move. Help me ... my leg hurts something awful!"

The splintering of the wood as they battered down the door was echoed in the pain shooting through my leg, the shouting of instructions, the hammering, and the fear that now caused my gut to knot up even worse. "Oh, God!" I screamed. "Help me!"

"All right, throw out your gun!" yelled a voice from the doorway of the bedroom.

"I don't have a gun! I'm hurt! I need help ... please!" I cried.

"Come out with your hands above your head!" ordered another voice.

"I can't! I've been shot in the leg, and I'm stuck in the doorway!" I yelled back.

Leaning over as far as I could stand it, I turned my head back toward the direction of the voices. There stood three men. One was pointing what looked like a sawed-off shotgun at me, and the other two leveled their pistols in my direction.

"Are you alone?" one questioned, as he edged closer.

"Yes," I groaned, before collapsing on my side.

At this point, I could care less about the guns. I needed a doctor. I felt sure I was going to bleed to death. Surely, I thought, I'd wake up any second, and this horrendous nightmare would come to an end. It didn't.

"We need medical assistance in here—got a man down," said one of the officers into his walkie talkie.

Two paramedics entered the room. They checked my vital signs then slowly placed me on a stretcher.

"Easy now," he said to me, "we'll have you out of here in no time."

Well, at least that's what he thought.

As we headed down the hallway to the elevator, dozens of glaring people lined the hallway. I felt so dirty, so ashamed.

Halfway into the elevator, the medics discovered the stretcher was too long to fit.

"Oh no!" complained one cop. "Can you take him off that damn thing 'til we get him downstairs?" he asked.

"No way! That leg has been moved enough already!"

"Sonofabitch!" muttered one cop to another. "All right then, there's only one thing we can do! Lieutenant," he spoke into his walkie talkie, "we're gonna need the hook and ladder truck. Stretcher's too big for the elevator. Subject will have to be lowered over the edge!"

The pain was excruciating as I was lowered over the balcony. Each time the cable stopped with a sudden jolt, I moaned, "Oh-h-h!"

And yet, I was just glad to get away from the eyes of my accusers, who now lined the apartment balconies to watch the show.

Following a short ambulance ride, the emergency doors of a nearby hospital swung wide open as they wheeled me inside. I was placed in a brightly lit hallway where I waited to be seen by a physician.

The next thing that happened almost blew my mind! Who did they wheel in and place on the stretcher right beside me but big John, the guy who had just tried to blow out my brains.

And my still-intact brain was running wild. I thought sure he was about to finish me off. My paranoia was intense.

I turned my head away from him and faced the wall. For a moment, I thought my teeth were chattering because the air conditioning was so cold. But I knew it was because I was afraid of the guy now lying beside me.

The glass doors opened a few feet away and a tall man in a suit pointed toward me and said, "What in hell is that guy doing beside the other one?" I quickly realized he was a police officer. He looked to a nearby nurse and asked, "Where can we move this fellow?" The nurse helped the officer push my stretcher into a side room.

Two young detectives came in, and the older, nicer officer left the room. One of the detectives read me the Miranda Rights. I must've blown their minds when I naively waived my rights, then proceeded to give them a full confession on tape. Of course, my admission of guilt was full of lies, sufficient to cover Tom's tracks. And yet, what did it matter to them? As far as they were concerned, they had their bird.

Deep down, I knew I hadn't been coerced into taking part in this crime. I had chosen my path, so why not take the rap myself? And on top of all that, there's that unwritten code among criminals: "Thou shalt not snitch."

Following my interrogation, I was surprised when both cops walked out, leaving me alone. An older nurse soon walked in with a clipboard and said, "Since you're a transient and have no insurance, we won't be able to treat or admit you here. This is a private hospital. They're going to take you somewhere else."

So, I was taken by ambulance to Broward General Medical Center in Fort Lauderdale, Florida.

There I was placed in traction in a five-bed ward on the third floor. Thankfully, I was quickly medicated, and maybe it was my imagination, but it sure seemed like the nurse used more force than necessary when jabbing the syringe into my bottom.

To place me in traction, my pants had to be cut off. This left me completely without clothes. I had no money, no family nearby, no friends, not even nearby acquaintances. For the first time in my life I was truly alone, except for the one-on-one, 24-hour guard, and he did nothing to help my loneliness. He probably had his own family at home, and besides, he was just there because he was working.

I was afraid. I was ashamed and angry. I was depressed, paranoid, and confused. I continually pondered how I could have been so stupid to get caught up in something like this and to have begun hangin' out with these types of people.

The heaviest thing on my mind was my dear parents back in Memphis and how hurt they would be when they found out. My wonderful parents had worked so hard to provide my two brothers and me with things they could never afford when they were growing up—things even some of our friends never enjoyed.

I seldom thought about my parents during my fast days of high living in Aspen. But now I did, and I didn't want their tender hearts to break.

I wanted desperately to crawl into a deep, dark hole and disappear. I wanted to die. For me, life had ended. To me, there was no hope for tomorrow.

As the medication began to take effect and I drifted off to sleep, my thoughts turned to Aspen.

It's been said that people cry out to God while in foxholes and prisons. Psalms 107:9-12 paints a vivid picture

of why it often takes a person to get knocked down before he or she will look up: "For He satisfied the thirsty soul, And the hungry soul He has filled with what is good. There were those who dwelt in darkness and in the shadow of death. Prisoners in misery and chains, Because they had rebelled against the words of God, and rejected the counsel of the Most High. Therefore He humbled their heart(s) with labor; They stumbled and there was none to help."

I had spent 29 years in rebellion, and when I was rebelling against my parents and the law, I was actually rebelling against God, whose Word reminds us "pride comes before a fall and a haughty spirit before stumbling" (Proverbs 16:18).✞

CHAPTER 2

TWO TYPES OF SNOW

"Hey man, you're ready for some longer skis … you were made for this sport!" encouraged Fred.

I had met Fred while shooting pool at Andres in Aspen. While Fred was an admitted ski bum down from Iowa for the season, I had actually moved there from Atlanta, Georgia, deciding to make this breathtaking resort my new home. Following several nights of playing pool, Fred and I decided to split the cost of a small house trailer outside a nearby town called Basalt. While it didn't look like much, our new home proved much cheaper than the short-term housing available in and around the more expensive Aspen. Our trailer was situated in a small mobile home park that overlooked the beautiful Roaring Fork River. This small river runs north to Colorado Springs and south past Aspen.

It was mid-November and the snow ski season had officially opened. I had never before skied, so my new roommate offered to introduce me to the sport. We chose Aspen Highlands for my first adventure atop the cold, white powder. This particular ski mountain is located between the more expensive Aspen slopes and a newer ski mountain called Snowmass.

Arriving early, Fred first suggested I learn to "turn" while using real short "boards" designed for beginners.

"Don't I need ski poles?" I asked Fred.

"Not yet; first I'm going to teach you to turn by traversing the hill. Once you get that down we'll put you on some longer skis and you'll have poles with them," Fred instructed.

"What does traverse mean?" I asked.

"It means you'll ski back and forth across an area of snow and you'll only turn at the edges," Fred patiently replied.

"What are edges?" I asked.

Sporting a wide grin but not laughing at me he said, "Here, just follow me and I'll show you how it's done."

Not an hour later Fred shouted, "Hey man, you're doing great! You're a natural at this sport. It's time for some longer skis and we'll go to the top!"

After exchanging my beginning "boards" for some long skis that he called 160s, we headed for the first ski lift. "How come your skis are so much longer?" I asked, as we sat down on the lift seat and were abruptly swung into the air.

"The length of your skis is best determined by your height and skiing ability," Fred responded.

We jumped off the lift at the top of the mountain. Fred slid smoothly down the small hill while my skis went one way and I went the other. "Ai-i-e-e-e-e-e-e-!" I screamed as I flew headfirst into a pile of snow. All I could hear was the muffled sounds of laughter as my face was now buried in the freezing snow.

"Here, take my hand and I'll help you up," offered Fred as he tried his best to stop laughing. "Sorry, I forgot to teach you how to get off the lift."

"Oh thanks," I stammered as I faked a swing at him, then fell right back into the frigid snow. Then we both laughed.

"Hey, where are we going?" I asked.

"This is only the first lift … we've got two more to go before reaching the top of the mountain," Fred responded.

"The *top* of the mountain?" I demanded, as lift number two swiftly lifted us high into the air. Then I looked back over my shoulder and shouted "*Look* at that view!" Never had I seen anything so breathtaking. As a soft flurry of snowflakes began to gently fall on my face, all I could see was beauty; hundreds of yards of solid white, with tall, green Aspen trees decorated with glistening ornaments of white snow.

"Wow!" I exclaimed "look at that! It's beautiful!"

"Those are the Maroon Belles," responded Fred.

"They're incredible" I sighed. "What are they?"

"The Belles are the mother of Aspen's wilderness areas," Fred continued. "If you look real close ... there on the right side ... you can catch a glimpse of Crater Lake! The water is crystal clear and shines like glass when the sun hits it."

Fred paused, absorbing the scenery, before pointing in another direction. "And over there is the Old Snowmass Ghost Town."

"Why do they call it that?" I asked.

"They say all the ghosts of dead skiers live there," he answered.

"Dead skiers!" I stammered.

"Yeah, the skiers who lose control their first day on the slopes, slide off into the trees and are never found," said Fred.

"You're lying!" I demanded.

"Yep," said a smiling Fred as he dodged my flying backhand, causing our lift to swing wildly.

"Whoaaaaaa," I screamed.

"Settle down, rookie," demanded Fred, "or you'll have us both in the hospital!"

Our chair lift continued to glide slowly through the air, and neither of us spoke for the longest time as we took in the views. Our quiet reflections were suddenly interrupted by Fred, who said "Here, take a hit off this!" He handed me a lit joint of grass, which I placed between my lips and slowly inhaled.

A short time later I sighed, "Man, this place is unreal."

"Yep," Fred replied. "Welcome to Aspen."

Finally, we reached the top of the mountain, and somehow I managed to stay upright as I slid off the short hill.

"Look over there!" I motioned to Fred. "Look at them catching that air!" A line of skiers was taking turns hitting a short jump.

"Let's go" demanded Fred, and I followed him to the jump. Moments later I took my first jump and I instantly knew I was in love with this sport.

"This is *fantastic*!" I shouted as I slid across my first hill.

"Don't forget what I taught you" warned Fred. "Take it real slow, especially on the edges, and turn slowly," his voice echoed as I headed down the mountain.

"This is a piece of cake," I thought to myself as my speed increased. Then it happened

"Look out!" came a scream from behind. I barely saw the silhouette of the skier as he flew by me, missing me by inches!

The close call caused me to lose my balance, sending my body one way and my skis another. Before I knew it, I was deep in the loose powder that bordered the groomed slope, my body flying forward at breakneck speed. The last thing I remember before hitting the tree was extending my arms straight out in front of me. Thankfully, this seemed to cushion the impact, as my right shin connected with the Aspen. Pain raced through my body as I fell back into the snow.

"Did you see that?!" screamed a voice from above.

"He had to have broken his leg!" responded another voice.

Grimacing, I opened my eyes and saw that the ski lift was right above me, loaded with skiers. So in addition to my pain, I was overwhelmed with embarrassment. It didn't matter that my face was covered by a ski mask and nobody could recognize me anyway.

From deep within I mustered the strength to straighten my legs and stand up, wrapping my arms around the tree for support. I determined that my leg was miraculously not broken and took one cautious step, then another, toward the groomed slope several yards away. I made it to my first ski pole before collapsing. Using that pole as a crutch, I searched for and found my other pole, which was right beside my other ski. Lying down in the snow, I managed to snap the skis into my heavy ski boots and then use my pole as a crutch to stand up again. I brushed the snow off my pants and jacket and took off! I flew across the slope and was able to maneuver at the edge. There I somehow was able to turn and stop.

"First time up?" questioned a voice from right behind me.

Embarrassed, I quietly muttered, "Yeah, and it may be my last."

The voice belonged to a beautiful lady with a striking figure made more obvious by her tight-fitting ski outfit. She encouraged, "When you traverse the mountain, don't point your skis so much downhill; you won't cover as much ground, but you'll fall much less. And don't worry about what others think ... we all started as beginners," she added. Her smile helped to decrease my embarrassment as she gracefully slid on down the slope, making it look so easy.

Aspen's Famed and Historic Jerome Bar

"This place is packed!" I yelled to Blue as we stacked boxes of long-necked Budweiser on a dolly before wheeling them down the hallway back to the Jerome Bar.

"Yeah" said Blue. "Winterschol gets as busy as Mardi Gras down in New Orleans, although that party lasts a week and ours is packed into one day!"

Like Fred, I had also met Blue while shooting pool at Andres and learned that he, too, was from Memphis. I later learned Blue worked two jobs, cleaning the Jerome Bar every morning and sometimes moonlighting as a disc jockey for local parties. But his major source of income was selling cocaine. Blue offered me a job to substitute for him when he couldn't clean the bar, and I jumped at the chance, especially when I discovered I could collect as much as $50 in change and even bills off the floor. "Once I found a hundred dollar bill!" boasted Blue. "It was rolled up in the shape of a straw and someone probably used it to snort coke!"

Winterschol is Aspen's annual non-stop party, complete with a parade. All the "locals"—people who actually lived and worked in the area year-round—dress up in costumes for this event. You could easily tell them apart from the "turkeys"—a name given to the tourists who flocked to Aspen for skiing and mountain sports.

On the morning of Winterschol, Blue asked me if I'd like to make some extra cash by helping him as a barback, and I quickly accepted. Barback is another name for "gofer," so it was our job to make certain everything was kept stocked, including beer, wine, and liquor. Despite the hard work, it was well worth it because working in Aspen was like driving a Cadillac instead of a Chevy! Until then, I had worked as a waiter up at New Snowmass, but I soon learned that all the best money was being made by those who worked in Aspen, where the most popular "watering holes"—another name for bars—were usually packed.

"Hey, Country Boy!" yelled a grinning bartender, "We're running short on Bloody Mary mix. Can you bring some up?"

"I'll be back in a flash!" I responded as I flew out the door.

"That guy is fast!" said James Perolle. "We oughta add him to our team!"

"I've been watching him," quipped Michael Solheim, as he returned his glass of scotch to the napkin set before him and took a drag off his imported cigar. Michael Solheim was the owner of the Jerome Bar, the most popular spot in Aspen and notably the hangout for all the visiting celebrities as well as the rich and famous who made Aspen just one of their homes.

The Jerome Bar was part of the infamous Hotel Jerome, an ornate and plush fixture that had been built in the late 1800s. It was specifically built to cater to the miners who had made Aspen their temporary home while feverishly working to strike it rich panning for silver in the nearby mountain streams. The three-story building also housed several shops and the popular Sayat Nova Restaurant.

That day I made over $80 in tips, but more importantly I caught the eye of the owner and his staff—easily the best bartenders in town!

The next day I was offered a bartenders' position at the Jerome. "Now Philip," said owner Michael Solheim, "we're going to start you off with one shift per week, but you'll also be the number one sub. You work hard—and demonstrate that high energy you showed us yesterday—and it won't be long before you'll be full-time."

"Thanks, Michael," I excitedly replied, "you won't regret this!"

Sure enough, three months later I was working full-time at the Jerome, as well as a part-time disc jockey on the weekend graveyard shifts at KSPN-FM, a radio station located in the basement of the Jerome Hotel. My life in the fast-lane had officially begun. Fellow bartenders and customers from the Jerome routinely stopped by the radio station to kick back and help me choose the music. And they always brought gifts; lines of cocaine to snort along with shots of Stolichnaya, a brand of Russian vodka.

One night, the Jerome was packed with people lined up three-deep waiting to place their orders at the bar. But of course we gave highest priority to our best customers, the locals who lived in Aspen year-round and especially the guys and gals who worked in the many other bars around town. It was a common courtesy to make sure we tipped each other something extra, especially for the drinks that we gave them "on the house."

"Hey, Hunter," I welcomed one such regular, "how are things down in Woody Creek?"

"What's shakin', Wild Man?" responded Hunter S. Thompson, a local who lived down valley on his ranch. I set his usual drink—a Chivas scotch on the rocks—on the bar in front of him.

"Just the usual," I responded. "Peace, love, and rock 'n roll!"

And while folks often called me "Wild Man," it was Hunter S. Thompson who wrote the book on being wild. Known as the "Gonzo Journalist," Hunter was best known for writing a column in the Rolling Stones Magazine, as well as such books as *Hell's Angels* and *Fear and Loathing in Las Vegas*. Rarely did I see Hunter when he was not high or drunk, or somewhere in between! Some of Hunter's best friends were Jimmy Buffet, another local, as well as a number of actors, authors, and film producers.

"Hey, Hick!" demanded an arrogant voice from the other end of the bar, "we need two more drinks here, and make it fast!"

The two guys who had been parked there all night were getting a little obnoxious, and everyone including the waitresses, fellow bartenders, and several customers knew it. And not only had they not tipped us, they had been acting like jerks. It was after 1:30 A.M., and we had already given the "last call for alcohol," when the inevitable happened.

"Hey, Hick!" yelled the same guy. "We need two more beers!"

"I already gave last call, and you didn't say a word," I said.

I had to duck as the guy hurled a handful of olives at me. Next, we all heard a scream come from one of the loudmouths after he was blindsided by a bar stool that sent him crashing to the floor!

Hunter didn't bat an eye as he turned to the guy's friend and calmly said, "If you don't want your face broken I'd suggest you get out of here—NOW—and take this piece of trash with you!"

With fear filling the guy's eyes, he lifted his so-called friend off the floor and half dragged him out of there.

"Hey, Hunter!" I yelled, "I think it's time for a shot and a line!"

"You're absolutely right, Wild Man!" he responded. "This party's just getting started!"

Soon after the last customer was ushered out (except for some of the locals) the party began! We partied until dawn, when Jimmy Buffet and Hunter went out to pick up breakfast, including Eggs Benedict, for everyone. That was a favorite breakfast, served special at Andres' Restaurant—a poached egg atop a piece of Canadian bacon and smothered in hollandaise sauce. But on this particular morning, none of them got eaten.

Just before Hunter and Jimmy left to pick up breakfast, we all dropped some windowpane acid, and our minds were coming off the wall by the time breakfast arrived. And speaking of "coming off the wall," the next day the bar janitor had his hands full, washing the dripping egg off the beautiful ornate mirrors that covered the wall behind the bar. Yeah, you guessed it: Everyone took part in an "egg toss" that left that place in shambles!

Our bar manager was named Tim Moon. One evening Tim and I were working the bar together when he introduced me to his friend Billy, who was visiting from Los Angeles.

"Hi Billy," I said as we shook hands, "pleased to meet you. What do you do for work in California?"

"Billy's an actor and also works as a mime," answered Tim. "But he also eats fire!"

"No way," I said. "Hey Tim, why don't we have him eat fire for our customers?"

"I don't know," replied a hesitating Tim. "Solheim might not like it."

"But he ain't here," I responded, "c'mon!"

A short time later I stood on the bar and made an announcement. "Hey everybody, we've got a real treat for ya'll tonight! Our friend Billy is going to treat you to some professional fire-eating!"

We did a fake drum roll on the bar, and then Billy amazed everyone as he repeatedly swallowed fire that he had lit on the ends of two sticks. The crowd went wild, and then they filled up a special tip jar we had set aside for Billy. We later counted $200 and gave it to Billy.

A short time later, I took a break and accompanied Billy to Andres Bar. "Hey Billy," I said, "Will you teach me how to do that? You made quite some change for just three minutes of fire-eating!"

That night, not only did Billy eat fire again, this time at Andre's Bar, but so did I! And at the following year's celebration of Winterschol, Tim and I dressed up as clowns. We were such natural clowns that afterwards locals asked us to entertain at their parties, especially for their children's birthdays. And on special events, when they were budgeted, they'd also hire me as "Klumsy, the Fire-Eating Klown!" I had added one more hat to my workaholic lifestyle.

✞ ✞ ✞

Later that night back at the Jerome, my fellow bartenders alternated shooters and beer while Tim counted the tip money.

"Here's yours, Hicks ... 200 bucks! We decided to give you a larger share after you ate fire for our late-niters, and they packed the tip jar!"

"Cool, man," I responded. I stuffed the money into my pocket and turned to leave the bar.

"Hey, Wild Man," yelled a waitress by the name of Rebecca, "don't rush off ... I'm having a party at my place and you won't want to miss some fresh hashish that arrived from Turkey!"

"Naw, not tonight," I answered. "Joyce is waiting up on me and we're gonna watch a movie. See y'all tomorrow."

I had lived with Joyce for nearly two years. The beautiful daughter of a Baptist preacher from Fort Payne, Alabama, Joyce had faithfully stuck by me despite my battles with drugs and my wild lifestyle. Not that she wore a halo, but she was a down-to-earth wonderful lady with strong character. She even had me going to church with her, but mere church attendance did nothing to change either my heart or my lifestyle.

Our friendship was headed downhill, largely due to my insecurities and jealousy. Joyce would often come to the Jerome and sit at the bar, just to see me. Then I'd get jealous when guys would talk to her, buy her drinks, and try to hit on her. This usually resulted in heated arguments later at the apartment.

Jimmy Buffet's Wedding

A few months later, around 200 highly-coveted invitations were personally distributed to the #1 Parrothead's wedding! Followers of Jimmy Buffet's music were called "Parrotheads," which linked them to his songs about pirates, sailing the seas, drinking, and drugs. I was floating in the clouds the day my invite arrived.

I was working the day shift at the Jerome and drinking Bloody Mary's with Hunter S. Thompson. I don't know who was more loaded, him or me, and I was getting paid to get high.

"Hey, Hunter" I excitedly asked, "Can I catch a ride to the wedding with you and your family?"

"Wouldn't have it any other way, Hicks," he responded, "but we're gonna leave early so we won't miss any of the action down at the castle!" Part of the reason I wanted to attend the wedding was because it was being held at a famous castle down valley from Glenwood Springs.

"What's the story behind this Redstone Castle?" I asked.

"Well," began Hunter, "it sits on 150 acres by the river, has 42 rooms, each one filled with valuable antiques. The place was built by a rich guy named John Osgood, who made his bucks in coal and steel. He wanted a place to impress his wealthy friends—people like John D. Rockefeller and Teddy Roosevelt."

"And now, *us*!" I yelled, lifting my mug to celebrate with a toast.

A few days later I found myself in the back seat of Hunter's Saab, sitting beside his young son, whose mom, Sandy, was in the front seat. Hunter was at his best, already high on something and taking deep draws on his cigarette, which he always smoked in a long cigarette holder.

"Here, Philip," said Sandy in a strained voice as she passed me a lit joint.

Personally, I couldn't relate to them smoking weed in front of their child, but such was the life in Aspen, Colorado. It was one of the most liberal cities in the world, and, seemingly, everyone embraced a philosophy of "peace, love, and rock and roll," regardless of their age or ethnicity.

Once we arrived at the Redwood Inn in Redstone, we parked the car and waited our turn for the horse-drawn carriage that would take us to the historic castle.

"Hey, Jeff! Hey, Jimmy!" I yelled as a limousine pulled up and several people piled out. "Looks like the Nitty Gritty Dirt Band has arrived!" Several musicians lived in the Aspen area, including the Dirt Band, John Denver, Don Henley, Glenn Frey, and Buffet. On that particular day we would be treated to one of the most amazing "jam sessions" ever assembled, as rockers such as Jackson Browne, Dan Fogelberg, Frey, Henley, Buffet, and others all joined in.

"What's say, Wild Man," asked Jeff Hanna, a musician with the Nitty Gritty Dirt Band, "got any refreshments?" As soon as we arrived at the Inn, Barry Cox, a fellow bartender from the Jerome, had pulled me aside and given me a sack filled with grams of cocaine.

"Here, Hicks," said Barry, "you're on the refreshment committee. Pass these out to the guests and, of course, be sure to partake yourself!"

While riding in the carriage from the Redwood Inn to the Castle, the party had already started as grams of coke were passed around, as well as a bong filled with Turkish hash. By the time we arrived, we were all floating and couldn't stop laughing.

Quite frankly, I gave out very little of the "refreshments" that day and consumed so much coke my heart and mind were racing. I was so high I began to get paranoid. Every time I talked to anyone, my mind played games. I just *knew* everyone was staring at my eyes, since my pupils had shrunk to the size of pinheads after snorting so much coke. I later feared that everyone was an undercover narcotics agent out to bust me. Truth was, everyone was just as messed up as me!

The jam session began after Jimmy and Janey, a South Carolina southern belle whom Buffet met in college, exchanged vows. Shortly thereafter I found myself riding alone in the carriage back to the Redwood Inn, before hitchhiking back to Aspen. It wasn't the first time that coke made me so paranoid that I ran away from reality.

Le Cabaret

After too many nights of my register coming up short, I lost my job tending bar at the Jerome. Of course I was guilty, as were other employees whose drug habits were more costly than our incomes.

A new club called Le Cabaret was opening in Aspen. Owned by a man from the Middle East name Gabe, it featured live bands and usually a comedian to open the bill.

I was hired as co-bar manager and teamed up with a fellow from Marin County, California, named Ed Hoban. I soon became close friends with Ed and his beautiful girlfriend, Nancy, who was once crowned Miss Utah. Nancy's beauty was matched by her gentleness. I soon learned she was the more mature of the couple, and Ed's wild personality needed her as a stabilizing influence.

"Philip," said Ed one afternoon, "I want you to meet our new comedian, a friend of mine from California. This is Robin Williams."

As we shook hands, Ed continued, "Robin, this is our good friend, Philip Hicks. He's a real decent guy."

I found Robin to be very quiet and rather shy—that is, until he got on stage, and then he became a totally different person. Off-stage, though, he usually reverted to being soft-spoken and low-key, especially when he was high. One night the crowd at the Cabaret overflowed the bar during intermission, and as usual, Ed and I owned the room—keeping our customers both high and entertained! Often Ed and I would do shots of tequila or Stoli just to keep up with our customers. And on this particular night, we were entertaining the crowd by "shooting flames" of 151 rum! To do this, we each filled our mouths with a shot of rum and held a lit cigarette lighter in front of our mouths. Then we spewed the rum through the flame, causing a long flame to shoot high into the air. Our favorite stunt was to stand at opposite ends of the bar and blow the fire toward each other at the same time so the flames would crisscross. The people would go bananas, and then they would routinely cram lots of cash into our tip jars!

One night I was wearing one of my favorite shirts. Called a "Nik Nik," it was made of silk and, with it, my cool looking silver and turquoise necklace. Someone counted us down, and on "three" we shot the flames across the bar. However, that time some of the rum dripped from my mouth onto my shirt and the flame ignited my chin then continued to my shirt!

"Owwwwww," I yelled as I ran to the center of the bar where two sinks were filled; one with clear water and the other with soapy water to keep the glasses washed. I dunked my head into the water and extinguished the flame. The sad thing was the crowd thought it was all part of the show and they clapped and yelled and, of course, threw more money on the bar. Thankfully, I suffered only first-degree burns.

That night we all went to Ed and Nancy's new home down valley in a town called Old Snowmass. After drinking and getting high well into the night, Ed took me aside and said, "Wild Man, c'mon with me, I wanna show you something."

Following Ed into his spacious three-car garage, my eyes widened in amazement as I looked upon giant burlap bags stacked from wall to wall—and every one of them was filled to the brim with marijuana!

"What in the world!" I exclaimed. "Where did all this come from?"

Grinning from ear to ear, Ed said, "This is how we pay for our beautiful home! Every three months or so, we receive a tractor-trailer load of pot and keep it here until it's picked up by another truck! We make $20,000 every time we store it!"

"This is amazing!" I stammered.

"Yeah," added Ed, "and we get all the pot we want to smoke—free of charge! Here," he added, as he handed me a large plastic bag, "help yourself."

It didn't matter how many drugs I consumed, how much I drank or how plentiful the sex, the next morning I always felt lousy and empty.

And no matter how often I wore clown paint and made others smile, it did nothing to bring joy to my own heart!

Yes, I simply wore one mask after another, and life just got faster and faster.

The faster it got, the further I ran from God and my personal beliefs.

The further I ran from God's love and light, the darker my world and lifestyle became.

Little did I know that very, very soon I would hit bottom—and there would be nowhere to look but up.

And in my case it was literal, as I was about to take a trip to Florida, where life as I knew it would never be the same.✞

CHAPTER 3

SEEING THE LIGHT

Had someone told me I would lie in traction for six months, I would have called them nuts! Had someone suggested I would then be placed in a body cast and it would be over a year before I'd undergo corrective surgery, I would've thought them crazy. But both were to prove true.

The worst parts of those 365 days flat on my back by far, though, were the first nineteen. If ever there existed a personal hell on earth that surely must've been mine.

Because of pain from my injury, I was given continuous injections of Demerol. And because of my drug-filled past, this only proved to make matters worse. My waking hours were filled with paranoia. I thought everybody—the doctors, nurses, patients, cleaning ladies, everyone—was an undercover cop, secretly conspiring to drain me of information related to my crime.

The veins in my arms were so perforated by the I.V. needles that they began to collapse.

Once I awoke in the middle of the night, the I.V. needle having slipped out of my arm, my bed filled with solution, and me screaming because I thought I was drowning.

Because of the medication, I went one 12-day period without having a single bowel movement. To say the least, pressure was mounting daily.

To top it all off, Tom had paid someone to hire an attorney named Robert to represent me. The attorney later told me Tom wanted to make certain I wasn't going to snitch on him. Because of my paranoia, I thought he, too, was an undercover cop, and I didn't cooperate with him, either.

On his second visit, Robert told me to get in touch with Tom and tell him he needed $10,000 for a retainer fee before he would even consider taking the case. He may as well have asked for the moon!

As for me, I just wanted to come back down to earth. It seemed I'd been forever high on drugs. Little did I know what the next day would bring.

Unbeknownst to me, the nurses began cutting back my medication, occasionally substituting it with placebos. I learned that a placebo is merely sugar water given to humor a patient. In my case, they were trying to determine how much of my pain was real and how much emotional.

By the nineteenth day of my hospitalization, all I was receiving was sugar water, but I still complained of intense pain. Quite frankly, I just needed a fix.

The following day, my guard was removed. "They're putting you on ROR," he told me as he was leaving.

"What's that?" I asked.

"It means, 'released on one's own recognizance,'" he answered as he waved goodbye.

Of course, being in traction, I couldn't go anywhere anyway. But now I at least enjoyed the freedom to talk with other patients.

That very afternoon, a young man named Ken was transferred into my room and placed in the bed next to mine.

He wasn't even fazed when I told him I was a prisoner. We became friends and the day passed quickly. Nighttime arrived, and the curtain that now surrounded my bed only served to depress me. I was no longer on medication, so my mind became clearer. This only made my anxiousness and fears worsen.

Thoughts of my parents drove me to tears that night, as they did every night. At that time my parents were unaware of my situation and whereabouts.

To be honest, they had begun to lose track of me during high school. As a senior, I got along well with everyone. One day I'd run around with the athletes, the scholars the next, followed by the church people, and finally, the delinquents.

Like many young people, I rebelled against my parents, figuring they were a couple of old fuddy-duddies who were trying to enforce the rules of their generation on me. The tighter the rules became, the more I rebelled.

In 1967 I graduated from Memphis' Frayser High School. Various jobs over the years had enabled me to finance my motorcycles and save for college.

I traveled to Murfreesboro for my first year of college, where I continued to make friends easily while attending Middle Tennessee State University. After being elected president of my class, the fraternities began pursuing me for membership.

That marked the beginning of my downfall; it was then that I began worshipping at the altar of "wine, women, and song."

I satisfied a mental desire to one day work as a journalist by becoming the sports editor of my college newspaper. To satisfy the emptiness in my soul, I joined three different church groups. And to pacify my body, I strove to out-party everyone, drinking and smoking pot excessively.

In 1969 I returned home and enrolled at Memphis State University, where I served as sports editor of the student newspaper as well as assistant to the Sports Information Director in the MSU Athletic Department.

Before long I was accompanying the athletic teams on coast-to-coast flights, and the fringe benefits were many. I was housed in the finest hotels, drove new cars that had been loaned to the university by local car dealers, ate steaks daily with the athletes, and, most importantly, gained valuable experience in the field of sports publicity.

By the time I reached the age of twenty, I figured I had arrived. But while my head was floating in the clouds—due to smoking grass as well as pride in thinking I had succeeded—my grades suffered. I quit attending classes and I did not tell my teachers why; they were forced to give me failing grades. After three consecutive semesters of straight Fs, I flunked out.

For the next three years I served as head waiter at the local TGI Friday's restaurant. However, with financial success and media attention came deeper participation in the drug culture. It appeared I was driving in the fast lane for good.

I then moved to Atlanta, Georgia, and for the next two years I became a "workaholic." Before long I was writing for a local newspaper, promoting stock car racing, and moonlighting as a bartender. To try to satisfy the need for God in my life, I joined the Unity Church of Atlanta. But it didn't make any difference, as my lifestyle of drinking and drugs continued. I lived with a lady from Memphis named Bobbie. She began attending a seminar sponsored by the Psychic Science Institute. One night she came home real late and confessed to me she'd had an affair with the president of the Institute, who had lured her to his room with promises of his hiring her as his personal assistant. Her unfaithfulness to me was all it took to end that relationship.

I moved west to Aspen and continued to wander aimlessly. Over the next three years my life took a downward plunge, fueled by drugs and fast living. As the seasons changed, so did my personality; heavy cocaine use took its toll. I was blindly incarcerated by the cravings of my own body. I had to get away, and my path led to that fateful vacation in Fort Lauderdale.

My thoughts were interrupted by a voice calling, "Philip."

It was Ken in the next bed, who upon hearing my crying, had reached out and pulled back the curtain.

While I couldn't pinpoint it, there was something different about this young man from England, that is, other than his accent.

Ken began telling me a story about another young man who was once arrested. He was bounced around from court to court while being tried on different charges. Ken told me this person's name was Jesus Christ, the only prisoner who's ever been truly innocent of every single charge brought against him.

A short time later, Ken asked "if you were to die this very night, do you know for certain, without a shadow of a doubt, that you would go to heaven?"

It didn't take me long to acknowledge that I was headed straight for hell.

Ken then said, "Philip, Jesus loves you just where you are. You don't have to clean up your act before coming to Him. He wants to replace your depression with His peace, and most importantly, He wants you to know for certain that if you *did* die tonight, you will join Him for eternity."

Ken even backed up those promises by showing them to me, right in the pages of the Bible.[2]

Well, I had gambled on a lot of things in my life, and the way I looked at it, if God's word was true, and I turned him down, then I had everything to lose.

Then again, if it was true and I took God up on His offer, I had everything to gain! The bottom line was: I was at the end of my rope—one lonely, hurting person—and I sure could use a shot of that peace Ken had just told me about.

So I jumped right in. Why, I didn't even care if anybody was watching, as I reached out and grasped Ken's outstretched hand, then repeated a prayer he prayed.

"Heavenly Father," I repeated, "I know that I have done a lot of bad things. I have sinned against You, and I need to be forgiven. Jesus, I thank You that You died on the cross for me. Thank You for paying for every one of my sins. I open the door of my heart and invite You to come in. I receive You and

Your forgiveness into my life right now. Fill me with the Holy Spirit and empower me to live for You. Thank You for saving me! In Jesus' name I pray, Amen."

For the first time in my life, I got real with God. I prayed that prayer straight from my heart, not my head. I asked Jesus to come into my heart, to forgive me of every filthy, rotten thing that I'd ever done, then to forget them. And He did. Suddenly, I knew I was saved![3]

No, there were no sky rockets, no flashing lights, not even an angelic choir singing. There was just this incredible peace that no drugs had ever been able to give me.

And that was only the beginning.

The following evening my hospital bed was surrounded. Not by cops. Not by nurses and doctors. Not by attorneys. No, I was enveloped by people much, much better than all the attorneys in the entire legal system.

I was surrounded by ten very excited Christians. I later learned from Ken that they were from his church, Coral Ridge Presbyterian in Fort Lauderdale. They brought a birthday cake with one candle on it. And they brought presents. They were there to officially welcome me into the family of God, to celebrate my first birthday as a child of God. I was one day old!

It didn't take me long to discover that these Christians were for real! They didn't care that I had been arrested or what I had done. They reached out to me with a love like I had never before experienced.

Unfortunately, not everyone's love was as unconditional. My birthday party was going strong when Larita, one of my nurses, entered the ward. Larita, who was from Jamaica, was very religious and outspoken. Her eyes filled with curiosity, she approached my bed, speaking with a high accent, "Hi, what is all this?"

My new Christian sister, Phoebe, replied, "We're having a birthday party for Philip. Won't you join us?"

Larita responded, "Oh, how old are you?"

Phoebe excitedly said, "Philip is a brand new Christian! We're celebrating his first birthday as a child of God. He's one day old."

"A Christian!" Larita exclaimed. "Why, he's not a Christian—he's smoking a cigarette!" She might as well have slapped my face.

My heart instantly sank with a new awareness of guilt, but sweet Phoebe gently answered, "Why, Philip is only a new baby in Christ. And his relationship with Jesus begins in his heart. Anything in his life that God dislikes will be shown to him as he grows as a Christian. And as he matures, Philip will be given the strength to stop doing a lot of things. God looks on the heart, not our outward man. And we should try to do the same."

Larita began to speak but held her tongue, and abruptly left.

My new friend Phoebe then encouraged me: "We all have growing to do. Don't be mad at her for criticizing you. Instead, let's pray that Larita will learn that it's God's job to judge others, not our own."

The following day, Ken was transferred back to his original room on the fifth floor of the hospital. And while I knew I would miss him, my void was now more than filled! Most importantly, a new friend named Jesus now lived with and in me, and I was now surrounded by a brand new family of love.

Continuing in Psalm 107, after one stumbles and there is none to help, verses 13-14 read: "Then they cried out to the Lord in their trouble; He saved them out of their distresses. He brought them out of darkness and the shadow of death, and broke their bands apart."

In 1 John 1:9 we're promised that if we "confess our sins God is faithful and just to forgive us our sins and to cleanse us from all unrighteousness."

I learned that we don't have to first clean ourselves up before God will accept us. On the contrary, He loves us so much, that "while we were yet sinners" Jesus died for us! (Romans 5:8)

Despite all my faults and failures, despite all my years of rebellion, just like in the story of the Prodigal Son, our heavenly Father patiently waits on each of us to come home to Him.✞

CHAPTER 4

MAKING AMENDS AND NEW FRIENDS

Before beginning my new life as a child of God, it was my deep desire that my parents never discover my whereabouts. I didn't want to face them after once again breaking their tender hearts.

However, now that I was a new Christian, I wanted them to know. I thought it best to first contact my dad, so I wrote him in care of his office. The following are excerpts from his tear-stained letter back to me:

> Dear Son,
>
> I hope this finds you doing well, despite your circumstances. Your mother and I have worried about you for some time, having not heard from you.
>
> Quite frankly, sooner or later we figured something like this might happen to you. It's inevitable when a person chooses to take drugs. Yes, we knew about that, too.
>
> We tried our best to raise you properly. And yet, sometimes a man has to get knocked down in order to look up. I am thankful that you've finally decided to get serious about God. Keep in mind, if you give God 100%, He'll give you the same.
>
> It's good you wrote to me first. If you don't mind, let's not tell your mother about this, that is, until it's absolutely

necessary to do so. In fact, when you write us, mail the letters to Aspen, and ask Joyce to forward them here. Hopefully, since this is your first offense, you'll be given probation, and soon you can tell your mother what happened face-to-face.

Regarding an attorney, do you recall our policeman friend, Wayne? He was charged with manslaughter for killing a young black boy in Mississippi, who had shot at him first. Well, Wayne's family mortgaged their property in order to get $15,000 for an attorney, and then lost it all.

I can't see us doing the same thing. Thus, it'd probably be best to accept the services of a free public defender.

Keep looking up!

Love, Pop

I had barely finished the letter when I began to sob uncontrollably! I buried my face in my pillow for fear everyone would hear. For once again I was reminded how wonderful a dad I truly had, and no matter how much I had hurt him and my mom, he still loved me and desired only the best for me.

Guilt filled my mind before a peace began to come over me. For some unknown reason, I felt everything was going to be OK.

✞ ✞ ✞

One day I received a package that lacked a return address. In fact, no one had even signed the enclosed letter. Yet, I knew it had been sent by Tom, for it contained the few personal items I had left in Al's apartment. It also contained an unsigned letter from Al. Among other things, they had sent my address book, but they had cut out all names that would link either Al or Tom to me. In a way, they were cutting me off for good. In fact, I never saw or heard from them again.

But since I now had my address book, I began writing and telling others what had happened to me.

Two of my closest Aspen friends, Ed and Nancy, surprised me with a visit. The day they arrived, I determined in my heart I was going to lead them to the Lord, too.

"Nancy! Ed!" I exclaimed, as they walked into my room.

"What's happening, Wild Man?" said Ed, as he gave me a big bear hug.

Following a kiss, Nancy said, "Oh, Phil, we're so sorry this happened to you."

"Oh, it's gonna be fine, Nancy," I said. "I've got the Lord in my heart now and already, life is different."

"Yeah man," interjected Ed, "that's cool, and hey, guess what we brought you?"

"What's that?" I said.

"Could you go for a snort of coke?" whispered Ed.

Hesitating, I answered, "Well… uh… no, I'd better not… well, maybe just a little one wouldn't hurt."

So moments after pulling my curtain back to hide our activity, I soon found my mind, and conversation, right where it'd been for the past 29 years—in the gutter!

That night after my guests had left and I had come down from my high, I began to feel terrible. How in the world did I weaken like that, after telling God and myself I'd never again get high on anything!

I began silently praying, asking God to again forgive me and promising I'd never fall again.

I remembered what Phoebe had said to Larita: "As he matures, Philip will be given the strength to lay aside many weights." Somehow, her words made me feel much, much better.

As my days were now filled with correspondence, visits by new Christian friends and Bible study, time passed quickly. I had also befriended Kathy, one of my favorite nurses.

While I was deep in thought one morning, she walked through the doorway, saying, "Hey, I must be in the wrong room. I was looking for my friend Philip, who usually lights this room with sunshine! Today there seems to be a big, dark cloud in here."

"Oh, hi, Kat," I said.

"What's the problem, Gloomy?" questioned Kathy, as she dabbed iodine on the traction pin that went through my leg, right below the knee.

"I'm sorry, Kat," I mumbled. "I miss my girlfriend, Joyce. She wants to visit me during Christmas, but she can only afford the air fare. Motels are too expensive down here, not to mention food."

"Hey, wait a minute, fella," interrupted Kathy. "You've been telling me about the benefits of being a Christian, and how God will now take care of all your needs. Don't sell Him short.[4] Your present problem's been handled, too! Joyce is more than welcome to stay with Lee and me, and she won't have to worry about food either."

"Really? Do you mean that?" I excitedly questioned.

"We've got plenty to eat," she added as she left.

Once again, I was stunned by the way everything was falling in place. Those nineteen days of nightmares now seemed so long ago.

✝ ✝ ✝

Since my Pop and I had decided it best to keep my circumstances a secret from my mother, his hands were tied when it came to sending me even a little spending money for essentials. Thus, in order for God to prove Himself faithful, He had to supply them all. And I'm not talking about material needs only! God often supplied through people I'd only recently met.

My area of the hospital was understaffed, and often my hair would go for days without being washed. Also, my toenails, which now seemed so far away, were shooting toward a record length.

One afternoon, two hospital volunteers walked in with a mobile bed shampooer and stopped beside my bed. "Hello," my name is Geneva and this is Pat," began one of the ladies. "We were told there might be someone in this room who could use a good shampoo. Would that someone possibly be you?"

I was so shocked I found it difficult to respond. But I didn't have to, as Pat lifted my head while her co-worker slid the light blue plastic box beneath me and began to fill it with water. "Now doesn't that feel wonderful?" said a smiling Geneva, as she poured warm water over my soapy hair.

"I must be in heaven!" I shouted, as I grinned from ear to ear. From then on, someone made it a point to shampoo my hair at least once a week. And if that wasn't enough, Phoebe began giving my toenails and fingernails regular clippings.

Sure, I loved all this attention, but quite frankly I also found it humiliating. I hated that all these people were going to so much bother on my account.

Then again, I was learning that as a Christian I'd have to die to a whole lot of pride. It was working, especially when the nurses had to help me with the bedpan. Now that was embarrassing!

One new friend, Pastor Bob from Coral Ridge Presbyterian Church, asked me if I'd write others who were sick. I gladly complied, and he provided me with a list of folks who were ill. After all, as much as I was being given, the least I could do was try to cheer up someone else.

Pastor Bob pointed out, "Philip, in the Bible there's a passage of scripture that talks about God being a God of comfort, 'who comforts us in our difficulties so that we can, in turn, comfort others' (2 Corinthians 1:3-4)."

"Well, imagine that," I said.

"So," he added, "by lifting the spirits of others through letters and words of encouragement, you're actually fulfilling scripture."

"Hmmm, that means my walk is matchin' my talk, right, Preacher?" I asked.

We both laughed as he responded, "Right on, brother!"

"Although I can't yet walk!" I added. We laughed again.

✞ ✞ ✞

One person I wrote to turned out to be a young girl named Sandy, who was definitely experiencing a few problems of her own. Paralyzed from the chest down as a result of being hit by a car, her dad blew the entire insurance check and then deserted her mom to run off with another guy!

And if that wasn't enough, while Sandy was still hospitalized, her mom left her. Sandy shared in her letter that she'd like to talk to me over the phone.

Well now, miracles are one thing, but this seemed next to impossible. Even though I was no longer under guard, I was still in the ward where other prisoners were sometimes kept. There were no phones in our rooms, and the closest one was down the hallway at the nursing station.

"With God, all things are possible!" shouted the aide who later helped push my bed, traction and all, down the hallway to the telephone.

And that phone call to Sandy turned out to be only the first of many! Before long, I was being taken on nightly rides down the hallway to call Joyce in Aspen and whoever else I wanted to call.

The day Sandy came to visit me, her wheelchair was pushed by two of the nicest people I'd ever met, John and Beth Harber. It turned out John and Beth were retired farmers from Illinois who were now involved in something called a "ministry of helps." And boy did they help me!

I never saw them when they didn't lift my spirit to the ceiling. They were filled with so much love, peace, and joy.

"You are so very special," said John, during our first visit.

"You wouldn't be alive today if God didn't have a purpose for your life," added Beth.

"Your letter said just what I needed to hear, at just the right time," said Sandy, "and you sounded so happy over the phone, despite the mess you're in!"

Things like this happened over and over during my year in traction and the body cast, and little by little my faith grew. I began to truly believe that there was indeed hope for tomorrow.

✞ ✞ ✞

After Sandy was sent to a specialty clinic somewhere up north, John and Beth began visiting me regularly. They became the mom and dad that couldn't be with me.

During several visits, they brought a guy with them who was as crazy as me! His name was Brother Butch. Before long, the majority of their visits were spent encouraging all the other patients in my room as well as staff throughout the hospital. In fact, there were so many "Jesus freaks" coming in and out of my room, people must've thought we were having a tent revival!

All we needed was a gospel quartet.

While growing up I rarely "honored" my parents, and in fact, I took them for granted. Little did I know that God places a high priority on the importance of children both obeying and honoring their parents. If one does both,

he or she is assured life will be well for them and heavenly promises will be their reward.

It wasn't coincidental that my deep desire was for my parents to know I had finally begun a personal relationship with Jesus. Once I finally made contact with my dad, I saw him in a totally different light and honoring him came so much easier. Honoring his advice to accept a public defender in turn honored my heavenly Father. That was a real cool thing to learn.✞

CHAPTER 5

GIVING THANKS

During my prolonged hospital stay, I got to know folks from all walks of life, including a fellow patient named Big Jim.

I soon learned Big Jim worked as a bouncer in a local bar, one of the many jobs that I had also worked. Big Jim was also a prisoner, released on his own recognizance. He stood well over six feet tall and looked like he could bench press a full grown steer. He wore his hair in a pony tail and never shaved.

While playing backgammon with him one day, I told him all about my "experience" that had led to my getting busted. In my case, I had gotten busted in more ways than one!

To my surprise, Big Jim could describe to a "T" the guy who shot me! Not only his physical description—but a whole lot more!

"Hey man," said Big Jim, "the cat's name is John Apostolou but he also goes by John Dinellio and Johnny Apollo. He's from Detroit, but he's done work in New York and Miami. And check this out: The word on the street is the dude's done some hit work for the family!"

"You're kidding!" I replied, knowing that he meant the Mafia.

Big Jim then added, "Man, you don't have to worry 'bout this dude showin' up in court, and testifying against you. He's been rippin' people off right and left. Why, he even strong-armed one guy for three kilos of smoke right out of the dude's own van in the parking lot of Mr. Laff's. In broad daylight. It ain't gonna be long 'fore his number is up! Somebody's gonna take him out; you can believe that, cracker!"

Our conversation was interrupted by one of the aides, who said I had a visitor, so Big Jim rolled his wheelchair back over to his side of the ward, and I leaned back on my pillow. "Hello Brother," came a voice from the doorway. I glanced up to see Joanne Cancelo seemingly float into my room. Ken had brought Joanne with him during a previous visit and we instantly became friends.

Of the many new Christians who'd come into my life, she stood out for some reason I just couldn't put my finger on. She was always so mellow, so peaceful, and nothing ever seemed to shake her. In the weeks, then months, that passed, she became sort of like the sister I'd never had. And one thing I really appreciated about her was that she always seemed to believe in me.

"Philip, I've brought you a book to read, which I believe you'll really enjoy," said Joanne. "It's entitled *Joni*[5], and when you finish with it, please pass it on to someone else. I've got to run now. Some friends from church have asked me to go witnessing with them on the beach." After leaning over to give me a warm hug, she left.

"What a babe!" chortled Big Jim. "I'd sure like to take her out!"

"No way," I quickly shot back. "She's not your type! You spend an hour with her and you'll be turning your life over to God!"

"I'll say," said Jim, "one hour with her and I'd think I'd died and gone to heaven!"

"Aw man, get off it," I blurted, as I hurled my pillow the length of the room, smacking him squarely in the face. We both laughed.

Before long I was deep into reading my new book, and the story it told really did a job on my heart. I could hardly believe the living hell that this young girl named Joni was going through. And I thought that *I* had gone through some heavy stuff.

As I read, I quickly realized my experience was child's play compared to hers.

The story was about a young girl who was about to graduate from high school and seemed to have it all together. She had a good home with a nice family in the northeastern part of the United States. She was an exceptional athlete, and she and her sister enjoyed horseback riding, water sports, and spending warm afternoons at the lake.

During one particular lake outing, Joni had an experience that changed her life in one splash. After diving off a dock, she hit her head on the shallow bottom, severing her spine and leaving her paralyzed from the neck down.

She wanted to die as she went through repeated humiliations, suddenly having to rely on total strangers to feed her, bathe her, assist her with the toilet, and other embarrassing situations. She was once the picture of health, yet now she couldn't even scratch her own nose. She would have rather ended it all than live like that for the rest of her life.

One day someone told her about Jesus Christ and how He could replace her depression with peace and fill her heart with joy no matter what her circumstances. While at first Joni didn't believe it could work, she gave it a shot, and it took.

If her book didn't do anything else for me, it taught me this: One of Joni's favorite scripture passages came from a book in the Bible called First Thessalonians. It instructs Christians to "rejoice always, pray continually, and give thanks in all circumstances" (1 Thessalonians 5:16-18).

On the surface, those seem like pretty tough instructions to follow, especially the last one. But despite a seemingly unbearable situation, Joni actually did it. This revolutionized her life.

After reading her story, I spent a lot of time comparing myself to Joni. Sure, I thought to myself, my leg was broken, I was thousands of miles away from family and friends, I had no clothes, no money, no car, nowhere to live, no job, and I'd been lying in the same bed for over two months. And I, too, had to experience a lot of humiliating things as a patient.

Worst of all, I could easily spend a long time in prison.

And yet Joni would possibly never even walk again, while I would. Unless God chose to heal her body here on earth, she would spend the rest of her life in a prison-like wheelchair. I would serve my time, then I'd be out.

And I had at least enjoyed several years of life after high school, while Joni hadn't even broken the surface.

But still, here she was, giving thanks in *all* circumstances. And her obedience was making a difference in her life.

I could never do that, I thought to myself. It sounds impossible!

But one night I prayed and asked God to help me do this if it was really His will and if it could make a difference in my life like it had in Joni's.

And I began to try it. From then on, even when I'd accidentally knock over my smelly urinal in the middle of the night, soaking my bed, I would be reminded to "give thanks in all circumstances."

And after doing this for awhile, I began to actually see a difference in my attitude. I noticed I quit feeling sorry for myself, and as I took my eyes off myself, I began to see others and realize everybody had problems. I even stopped complaining! That had to be a miracle.

Once, the true test came. By this time my leg had been hanging in traction almost three months, held by a pin through my shin bone. One afternoon, the rope holding up the weights broke, sending my leg flying upwards!

"Yee-ow-ow-ow-ow!" I screamed, as nurses and attendants came running into my room. I lay back, grimacing in pain, holding my breath in an effort not to curse, and quietly, something came over me. I began to silently pray, and as strange as it seems, I began to say, "It's difficult, God, but I give thanks that this happened."

Suddenly, the intense pain began to slowly disappear.

The technician repaired my traction setup. After he left, Big Jim wheeled over and said, "Man, those idiots should have checked your rope more often. They ought to be shot!"

I responded, "Naw, man, it's all right, we're all human, and every one of us is gonna make mistakes. It's important that I forgive whoever was at fault, no matter who's at fault."

"What the ... ?" his eyes narrowed.

"Because," I added, "if I don't forgive others, then God won't forgive my own screw-ups."

Big Jim was speechless. He wheeled back over to his own bed.

Later, one of the Christian nurses told me that Larita, the nurse who'd previously questioned my Christianity because I was smoking, was talking in the break room and said, "That young man sure has changed. Why, I haven't even heard him curse anymore, and he was even praying for another patient this morning. Maybe he truly is a Christian now."

When I heard this, I couldn't wait to tell Phoebe, the sweet friend who'd stood up for me the night Larita had come down on me. And I got my chance the following day when Phoebe came by to visit.

"Phoebe! I'm so glad to see you," I exclaimed, as she walked into the room.

Smiling, as always, she responded, "Why, what on earth could it be? Are your charges being dropped?"

We both laughed, as she gave me one of her familiar squeezes, and I said, "No, no, nothing like that, but something super has happened, just the same."

Handing me a just-opened box of Russell Stover candies, she said, "Well, what is it, my little man of faith?"

"Joanne gave me a book to read called *Joni.* It's all about a young girl who became paralyzed after a diving accident, then got so depressed she wanted to kill herself. Then she became a Christian and soon after, started giving thanks in every situation," I quickly blurted out.

"Well, praise the Lord," Phoebe whispered.

"I thought she was crazy," I continued. "I figured it was ridiculous and even impossible for a person to give thanks when things aren't goin' his way. But as I continued to read, I saw how life for her began to change after that. In fact, she actually seemed much happier, even while she couldn't even move her arms, much less her feet!

"So, I figured, if this could work like that for Joni, then I wanted to give it a shot...and I did."

After telling Phoebe about the traction breaking and my conversation with Big Jim and what the nurse had said about Larita, Phoebe smiled from ear to ear and said, "Philip, I'm so proud of you. You've grown so much in such a short time. And now you've uncovered a spiritual truth that often takes Christians years to discover—and even then, they don't act on it. Many continue to live in defeat."

"I hope I've got all that," I said, grinning.

"Allow me to be more specific," she continued. "God's Word instructs us to 'do all things without complaining' and to 'rejoice in all things.' When a Christian does this from the heart, it allows God to release His power into their circumstances, and soon they see not only a change in their attitudes, but things also improve for them. When this happens, other Christians, like Larita, for example, observe them and see they're for real."

"Tell me more," I said.

"Where most miss the boat is, while they actually do begin giving thanks in the midst of adversity, they continue to complain. One cancels out the other, and this ties God's hands, preventing Him from working on their behalf."

"Oh my goodness," I said.

"And," she added, "when you begin praising instead of complaining, whether you realize it or not, you've gone through a transition of 'dying to self,' and when this happens, God is being glorified as Christ, through the Holy Spirit, and shines His light through you."[6]

"Well, how does God do that?" I asked, as I reached for another chocolate. "And why does He wait on a person to start giving thanks for something they don't like before He moves in to help?"

"Wait a second, brother, not so fast," Phoebe said. "You're not giving thanks *for* the situation, but you're giving thanks *in* it, or in spite of it. This is where a lot of Christians miss the mark. Thus, it doesn't work for them, and they wonder why. Psalms 22:3 reminds us that God lives inside our praises. In Hebrews 13:15, God reminds us that oftentimes it takes a sacrifice for a person to praise, and give thanks, yes, even when one doesn't feel like it. When someone steps out in faith and acts on this, God is honored and He supernaturally intervenes."

"All that is kinda hard to grasp, but I gotta buy it, 'cause I tried it, and somehow it worked for me," I said. "So as long as it keeps working, I'm gonna use it!"

"That's the attitude. Here, have another chocolate!" offered Phoebe. And I did.

John 1:12 reminds us "for as many as believe in [Jesus] to them He gave power to become the sons of God." In our own strength it's *impossible* to give thanks in all

circumstances and to quit complaining, but God promises to empower us to be able to "decrease" in ourselves so that He can "increase within us." Galatians 2:20 says "we're crucified with Christ and we live. Yet not us but Christ lives in us!" In our own flesh and strength, obedience is impossible, but in His strength we can live victorious lives.✞

CHAPTER 6

NEW HEIGHTS

A few days later, I was enjoying one of my favorite lunches when an unfamiliar voice asked, "Are you Philip Hicks?"

I hesitated for a moment. "Yes," I said, as I looked up into the serious face of a tall, slim man who was dressed in a stately three-piece suit. Truth to tell, in my present prone position, everyone looked tall to me.

"My name is Frederick Kaufman," he said, in a serious voice. "I am an attorney, and I've been hired by a Miss Joanne Cancelo to represent you."

"Sir, Joanne Cancelo works in a health food store, and she can't afford an attorney for me," I quickly replied. "Besides, my Dad suggested I accept the services of a public defender, 'cause there's no way of knowing how expensive this thing could get before it's over. And I have to agree with my Dad. I, too, think it's best to get a P.D."

"Well, Mr. Hicks," he responded, "I respect you and your father's decision to utilize the services of a public defender and wish you well. However, since I've already been retained for an initial consultation, why not go ahead and tell me your story? Then, when you're through, you can sign this form, releasing me of all legal representation."

I thought to myself, well, he seems like a pretty decent guy, and besides, Joanne did pay him to come here.

I replied, "Well, sure. Why not?"

As I began to describe what had happened to me, at times Mr. Kaufman appeared to be asleep, he looked so peaceful. But, he wasn't asleep, because every now and then he would acknowledge me with a silent nod of his head.

Finally, I was through, but he wasn't!

Little did I know that his brief response would prove to be words that would echo in my mind for days to come and would prove to cause a miraculous turning point in my life.

After signing the release, I shook hands with Mr. Kaufman, said it was a pleasure meeting him, and he walked toward the door. Then he stopped short, turned around, and came back to my bed.

"Mr. Hicks," said Mr. Kaufman, "I'd like to leave you with some advice."

"Sure thing," I responded.

Speaking with carefully chosen words that seemed to resonate with power, he said, "Mr. Hicks, please consider the following: Miss Cancelo's faith is such that she believes her heavenly Father will provide all the money she will ever need to pay for an attorney for you. That is where her faith stands."

While my faith wasn't expected to be too tall, I quickly got the point, and I immediately felt six inches tall.

However, his last statement was the straw that broke the camel's back—or, that broke my heart! "And secondly, you may as well forget about asking the Lord into your heart, and all of the peace and joy and these wonderful things that have been happening to you, if you don't go into that courtroom and tell the whole truth about everything. You don't owe anything to the guy who got away. Your life is now aligned with God's, and He has no room for those who'll compromise and not be willing to give Him their all. A person who is double-minded cannot receive anything from God."

Moments later, Mr. Kaufman left. But his parting words continued to ring in my mind, and then heaviness began to weigh down my heart. I began to silently cry.

"Oh, God," I quietly prayed, "I don't want to half-step you, I don't want to compromise, I don't want to be a phony. I just didn't think it was necessary to bring up the guy who was involved in this crime with me. Anyway God, all that happened before I became a Christian. And why do I have to be a snitch? After all, I chose to get involved in all this."

From somewhere deep within me came the words: "I'm not asking you to tell on anyone. I just want you to tell the truth, for only then will you truly be set free. That's all I want, my child, I just want you to be free."

It dawned on me that if I had gone to court, I may very well have lied about some things. And in doing so, I'd be acting no different than how I'd acted while living for the devil most of my life. Then I remembered something my grandpa once told me: "There's a difference between telling the truth and snitching."

And I was tired of playing games. I wanted to finally get real with God, go all the way, and show Him I meant business, to show Him this was not another case of "jailhouse religion."

Then I realized I had just blurted out loud, "OK, God, I'm gonna tell it all, no matter what happens, no matter how much time I get. I'm not going to worry about what comes down!"

"Are you through with your lunch tray, Philip?" asked a curious-looking Larita.

Not even caring how long the nurse's aide had been standing there, I smiled and happily responded, "Yes! And it was delicious."

By now she probably thought I had really gone off the deep end, for I had barely touched my plate.

✝

John 8:32 reminds us "Ye shall know the truth and the truth shall set you free." The Cross is both vertical and horizontal. When we begin our relationship with God, this is a picture of the vertical side of the Cross... when we get honest with Him and confess our sins. Then once our relationship begins, we must choose to be a "doer of the Word and not a hearer only," and this requires us to be honest horizontally—with our family, friends,employers, and others.

Yes, being honest can be difficult, even embarrassing. But God honors those who walk in His truth and are truthful with his or her fellow man.

Ask yourself this question... would you rather obey God or man?✝

CHAPTER 7

BABY STEPS

The days now seemed to fly by. Since the day of the attorney's visit I decided to tell the whole truth at my trial, no matter the outcome. It felt like a huge weight had been lifted off me.

And my attitude was changing, even toward the guards who often stopped by to check on me. Actually, they weren't supposed to check on me, since I was now released on my own recognizance. However, the only reason I was placed on this status was because they knew I couldn't split, even if I desired to do so.

This way the County saved bucks by not having anyone baby-sit me 24-hours a day. Even so, a great deal of publicity had surrounded my case, and the county wasn't going to take any chances.

"Hello, Mr. Hicks, how's that leg?" asked a particular sergeant during one supposedly unofficial visit.

"It's fine, just fine, thank the Lord," I responded, then awaited his usually snide remark.

"Still messin' with that religious crap?" he asked. "Only time will tell how long that stuff is gonna last. I've seen a lot of guys come through the county jail. Bunch of 'em get real religious, that is, until the judge sentences them. Then most of 'em git rid of that Bible quick!"

As I was about to respond to his sarcasm, in walked John Harber, who patted the guard on the shoulder, smiled that million dollar smile, and said, "You look real sharp in that uniform, sergeant. I hope you and your family enjoy a wonderful Christmas."

The sergeant, who was suddenly at a loss for words, looked sheepishly at the floor, muttered "Thanks," and quickly left.

"Boy! That clown makes me mad, John," I blurted. "Who does he think he is, always goin' around judging other people? He ain't got any room to talk, with all the garbage that comes out of him! How can you be so nice to him?"

"Now, brother," John said, "despite his uniform, he's a human being, too, and Jesus loves him just as much as He does you and me. We must face the reality of your situation, and remember it's only natural for people to doubt your conversion experience, even more so because it took place after you got into trouble. So try hard to ignore their remarks and pray that God will give you the grace to be nice to them—yes, even when they're mean to you."

"I don't know..." I hesitated.

"It's much easier to love those who are nice to you, but Jesus directs us to love even our enemies," advised John.[7]

"John, you make it sound so simple, and I see it work for you all the time. I get so frustrated when I can't make it work!" I said.

"Just relax. Rome wasn't built in a day, and it's going to take a while for life as a Christian to get easier for you; but it will, just you wait and see. What's important is for you to just rest and keep trusting in the Lord. In due time, He will enable you to do good things to even those who are mean to you."

"I'll try," I replied rather sheepishly.

"Meanwhile, don't feel bad when you mess up. We all mess up every single day," John added. He then handed me a package, gave me a bear hug, and left.

I opened the box, and then grinned from ear to ear. Inside was a brand new Bible, and it even had my name on the front.

As I clutched it tightly to my chest, tears rolled down my face, and I quietly thanked God for friends like John, who had become like a father to me when my own father was a thousand miles away. Yes, I was beginning to realize that God was more than an impersonal being far away on another planet. He was now my heavenly Father, my Dad, and He longs for personal fellowship with us.

Somehow, God really did know my needs, even before I asked. And yet, already He had been so good to me, that I didn't really feel right about asking for anything.

In time, I was to learn that every single promise in the Bible is meant for us to receive. We have to line up our desires with His desires first, then continue to walk in obedience.

We're reminded in 1 Peter 2:2, "as newborn babes [we are to] desire the sincere milk of the Word, that by it we may grow." Hence, if certain parts of the Bible are milk, then other parts are "Gerber's baby food," so to speak, and then meat.

And just as Brother John encouraged that "Rome wasn't built in a day," I was learning the importance of not trying to "grow up" too fast as a Christian lest I get "spiritual indigestion." I needed to build my house slowly, beginning with a solid foundation, so when tests and trials came, it would prove far more difficult to fall.✞

CHAPTER 8

THE TRUE MEANING OF CHRISTMAS

On the morning of December 24, 1978, I was awakened by two cheerful voices announcing that they were here to shampoo my hair. Two hospital volunteers, Geneva and Pat, had been treating me to weekly shampoos for almost a month, and it was proving to be one of the most wonderful experiences I had ever enjoyed. A person takes a shower for granted until that privilege is taken away.

For the longest time I had gone without my hair being washed. My scalp had become irritated and itched something awful.

Then one day, Geneva walked in and announced they had gotten permission to order a portable shampoo machine, which arrived the following day. It was fantastic!

"Your bed looks like a Christmas tree!" Geneva exclaimed.

"Yeah, and now Santa has sent two of his pretty helpers to wash my hair!" I said, while grinning from ear to ear.

I told them about the church group that had visited the night before, decorating my overhead traction bar and my bedside table with bows, ribbons, and the works. "If they could have gotten away with it, there'd be lights all over the room," I added.

"When is your girlfriend, Joyce, due to arrive?" asked Pat.

"She flew in from Aspen last week!" I excitedly responded. "Sure wish you could meet her. She's out shopping right now, but she'll return later."

"I wish we could, too" said Geneva, "but we have to visit another hospital this afternoon."

"Please say hello for us, and enjoy your last few moments with her," said Pat, as they headed out the door.

Three o'clock took forever to arrive, but I finally looked up to see my sweetheart of the past two years walk through the door.

"Oh, Phil," Joyce said, "I've been so worried about you, but now that I've seen and talked to you these past five days, I'm starting to believe that you really have had a change in your heart. I'm so glad your friends came by last night just to meet me."

Ken Rodway, the young man who had led me to Christ, and Joanne, the girl who'd hired the attorney to represent me, had visited the previous night. And before leaving, they had prayed the sinner's prayer with Joyce, too.

"How I wish I could take you out of this traction, even if just for a night. It's Christmas Eve, and you don't need to be in an old hospital bed. It just doesn't seem fair," Joyce said. "I know you've changed, why can't they just let you go?"

"Because, God has only just begun with me, Joyce," I said. "I've got a whole bunch of changin' to do before I'd be of any use to you, God, or anybody else," I added, as I hugged her goodbye and gave her one last kiss, as she would be leaving for the airport early the next morning.

"Now you be sure to write and tell me if you need anything," Joyce said before hurrying out the door, probably hoping I wouldn't see the tears in her eyes.

No less than eight more people dropped by before visiting hours ended that evening, and I later learned several others were turned away.

As I lay in bed, I began to think about all that had happened to me, and I, too, got misty-eyed.

I then began reflecting on the true meaning of Christmas, and I opened my new Bible to read about the story of when Jesus was born. It meant more to me than any other time of my life. Before that day, the story seemed so impersonal.

But now, here I was, separated from all the parties, all the Christmas shopping, even apart from my family for the first time in ages, but it didn't seem to matter. This night, a real peace came over me. I closed my eyes and began to silently pray, and then I heard them.

It sounded like angels singing, and their voices were getting louder and louder. I thought I was dreaming. I opened my eyes and realized this was no dream.

There, standing in the doorway of my hospital room, was a group of people singing Christmas carols. Their faces seemed to be glowing.

I could no longer hold back the tears. But they weren't tears of sadness—they were tears of joy.

This was surely the most wonderful Christmas of my entire life, because for the first time ever, my heart was right with God. And I finally knew the true meaning of Christmas!

Nothing else seemed to matter.

We're reminded in 1 Samuel 16:7 that "while man looks on the outward appearance [of others], God looks on the heart." And while Joyce had observed outward changes—in my conversation and appearance—and meant well in thinking the authorities should release me, our heavenly Father knew I needed to go through a refining fire to become more like Him. I had been in the fast lane for over 29 years and I needed much more time to slow down, much more time to die to self.✝

CHAPTER 9

THE EDGE OF THE DESERT

The holiday season was quickly over and February had arrived. My doctor had planned to perform surgery on my leg. However, the unofficial word was that the County had talked my doctor into postponing surgery so they wouldn't have to pay the huge bill.

So instead, I was placed in a body cast. It extended from my chest down to my right leg, with a type of stick holding my other leg in place. My doctor chose this particular cast because it served to stabilize my spine, limiting further damage to my right leg. It must have worked, because I felt like a mummy, only my pyramid was a Fort Lauderdale hospital room.

Little did I know that this, too, was about to change.

Throughout this time, I had continued to grow as a Christian. Some people didn't quite know how to take me, including Michael Hittleman, the young public defender who had been assigned my case. He was intent on doing everything possible to build a solid defense in my behalf, despite the odds stacked against me. I probably wasn't much help to him. In fact, my attitude was freaking him out. All I wanted to do was talk about God and what He had done in my life.

One thing I did mention to my P.D., however, was the conversation I had had with Big Jim, the former patient in my room. My P.D. seemed quite interested in what Big Jim had told me about the guy who had tried to take me out.

As a matter of fact, I later learned he had done some extensive investigating, talking to the County Jail officials and even the judge who was scheduled to hear my case.

A couple of weeks passed, and one day an ambulance arrived to haul me away.

"Where are we going?" I asked the officer who accompanied us.

"You're going somewhere where you'll be safe," he said.

"What do you mean 'safe'? I was doing just fine at the hospital. I don't understand," I said. But he would say no more.

The ambulance pulled into the parking lot of what appeared to be an apartment complex. They placed me on a stretcher and pushed me down a walkway. I couldn't help but notice the armed guards standing at each end of the sidewalk. Also, several guys were carrying suitcases and boxes out of the apartments, taking them to the building directly in front of this one.

They took me into one of the apartments, and there I was surprised to discover a hospital bed, complete with traction setup, exactly like my old hospital bed.

The medics and the officer left. A short time later, in walked a young man dressed in blue. "Howdy, my name's Ralph, and I'm gonna be your helper," he said.

"What's going on over here?" I questioned. "Why did all those guys move over to the other building?"

"Man, they ain't telling us nuthin'," Ralph said. "All I know is they asked for a volunteer to help take care of you, and they promised it'd be extra good time for me, plus I wouldn't have to go out on work release, so I jumped at the chance."

"What do you mean?"

"This here is a County Work Release Center, right across from the main county jail," Ralph added. "And get this—nobody is allowed to come near this apartment, except me and the guards!"

"What!? You mean I can't even have visitors?" I questioned. "Man, this is a real bummer!"

The next day, my P.D. dropped by to see me and clued me in on why I had been moved. It appeared that their investigation of the man who had shot me had turned up some information that confirmed what Big Jim had told me about the guy. And while they couldn't prove anything, they wanted to make certain he didn't try to slip into the hospital and take me out...or have somebody else do the job.

In other words, they felt I needed protection.

"But, God's not going to let anything happen to me," I assured my P.D.

"Well, that's probably so, but we're not going to take any chances, and besides, we're just assisting God," said my P.D.

"Nice of you fellows to be so considerate," I said.

"Now, I've arranged for you to have one regular visitor. Who would you like it to be?" he asked.

Now that part was easy. "John Harber," I said.

Thus began what seemed like a time in the desert compared to all the constant attention at the hospital—visitors, telephone calls, gifts, and on and on. But John's frequent visits proved to be a refreshing oasis.

There was no way I could have known that this desert was to prepare me for still another, which loomed right down the road.

Throughout the Bible we find examples of God's children having to endure "desert" experiences, and most of the time we learn these are not meant for bad but for good. It

is in our deserts that we are able to "be still" and hear God. If Jesus needed to take time away from others, then we need to follow his example and do likewise. A desert can help restore our souls and better prepare us for challenges that lay ahead.✝

CHAPTER 10

MANY MOVES

Two weeks later I went on yet another ambulance ride.

This time our destination was the Broward County Courthouse, where I was wheeled into an elevator and then taken into a large, ornate courtroom. Court was in progress, and you should have seen the gawkers after I was placed in the center of the aisle, not far from the judge's bench. Compared to the night of my crime, this time I didn't mind all the people staring. In fact, I realized it was only natural for them to do this.

As my public defender began discussing his motion with the prosecutor, I heard my name called out. I looked around, but couldn't pinpoint just who was speaking to me.

"Up here, Mr. Hicks."

I looked up and was quite surprised to discover it was the judge, clothed in a black robe, who had called my name.

"How are you, Mr. Hicks?" questioned the judge, who I later learned to be my trial judge, Joseph Price.

"Well," I hesitated, "uh, I'm just fine, Your Honor, just fine."

"Mr. Hicks, Ecclesiastes says 'to every thing there is a season, and a time to every purpose under the sun,'" said Judge Price. "What season do you think this is, Mr. Hicks?"

I immediately realized he had just quoted some scripture out of the Bible. And before I had time to even think, I responded, "Well, Your Honor, I guess this must be my season to go to court."

We both smiled, and I immediately knew I had no reason to be nervous.

My public defender presented a motion to suppress the recorded confession I made the night of my arrest, but that motion was denied.

Following my first day in court, I was returned to my room at the vacated Work Release Center. The next few weeks were filled with intense Bible study. Before long, I could quote scripture as if it were second nature.

Even Ralph noticed the difference. "Hey man," he said one day, "I ain't never heard nobody talk about the Bible like you do. Why, it even sounds interesting. And you don't come across like you're preachin' either. I hate it when them preachers try to shove that Bible down your throat; that makes me sick. But you make it sound fun!"

"Well, Ralph," I answered, "it is fun. And it sure makes a big difference when you don't *have* to read the Bible. Instead, you do it 'cause you want to learn about God! I can't quite understand it, but the words in the Bible even make me feel good inside."

John came by to visit later that day, and when he and I began to talk, Ralph joined in. "Hey Preacher!"

I chuckled, "Seems like everybody thinks John is a preacher, just because he always carries a Bible."

"Can anybody be saved? Er, I mean, even if a person has lived a bum life, even if they were doing B and Es for years?" asked Ralph.

"Why, Jesus went to the cross for all of our sins, Ralph, yes, even Breaking and Enterings," replied John, as he put his arm around Ralph's shoulder, smiled warmly, and asked, "Could you be talking about anybody we know, Ralph?"

Ralph stared intently at the floor, and muttered, "Yeah, I'm talking about me."

After John counseled with Ralph, we all joined hands, and John asked me to lead Ralph through the sinner's prayer.

Admittedly, this was a brand new experience for me, but once I got started, somehow I began finding the right words. Later I learned God isn't interested in fancy words. He just wants a person to pray from their heart. And on this day, Ralph did.

"Well, I don't feel no different," said Ralph, "but I'm kinda glad I got it off my chest."

"Well now, Ralph," assured John, "Christians don't go by feelings; however, often we certainly express our emotions. We walk by faith, and it's important now that you accept the Lord at His promise. He promises that if you confess your sins to Him, then He'll forgive them. What's that term? Wipe your slate clean! You asked, and He has! You can believe that!"

We all laughed.

"Hey John, you're getting pretty cool," I said. "You're starting to sound like us!" And we all laughed again.

✝ ✝ ✝

The next day, Ralph was released. I never saw or heard from him again, but we continued to pray for him, hoping he'd stick with it and get serious about God.

Before he left, I was introduced to my "next helper," a guy named Mike, who considered himself a real con man.

Before the week was out, he had filled me in on every crime he'd ever committed, and he was already bragging about his next planned theft.

Mike wasn't open to the Gospel, but he sure did take an interest in me.

"Hey dude," said Mike, "Man, you oughta file a case against these creeps. Man, they ain't giving you proper medical treatment a'tall. I know, 'cause I been in a prison hospital before, and I know what your rights are as a prisoner. Man, they're s'posed to have a real nurse available to you—24-hours a day! And, if you need medication, they gotta give it to you immediately!

"And besides, you got a bunch of inmates playing nursemaid to you. We ain't been trained to do this crap! You're s'posed to have your sheets changed regularly, get regular baths, and have lotion put on you so's you don't get bed sores. And man, I ain't doin' none of that crap! That crap is fer sissies!

"Man, I betcha' you got a case against the County, and if you play your cards right, they's liable to let you go, providin' you don't sue their butts. Ain't you never heard the term, God helps them who helps themselves?"

I couldn't wait to see John Harber, who usually came to visit me on Mondays.

"Hey, John!" I said, as he walked through the door, his hands full of the usual candy, envelopes, stamps, stationary, and other gifts.

"Hello, Brother," he responded.

"Look John," I continued, "this is a list of all the improper medical treatment I've been getting. If I sued them, then they might drop the charges against me. Whaddaya think?"

As usual, the first words out of John's mouth were, "Praise the Lord!"

And yet, John changed the subject, choosing not to advise me on a possible lawsuit.

✞ ✞ ✞

Two days later, my two armed chauffeurs picked me up once again. This time, they took me right across the street to the Broward County Jail. And what a reception I got!

There was the major, the captain, the sergeant who often made fun of religion, and around twenty new roommates.

As several people picked me up, stretcher and all, and tilted me almost vertical to get me up the stairs, the officers looked on with obvious concern on their faces. Suddenly, I got the idea that they didn't really want me in their jail. To say the least, my particular case was a first for them, and they certainly didn't have accommodations for prisoners like me. But they were getting their orders from somewhere.

It took me only a few days to figure out that their orders were coming from above ... way above. Later on, I came to the realization that my steps, or rather my stretcher, were being ordered and guided by the Lord.

(Of course, if you'd told me this six months earlier, I would have suggested you'd gone off the deep end.)

✞ ✞ ✞

My newest home turned out to be a large cell that housed the jail trusties, seventeen of them to be exact. And, you guessed it—one of them was assigned as my "helper.

Because of minimal floor space, my large hospital bed was wedged between two sets of bunk beds in a rear corner of the cell.

As usual, I became an instant celebrity. Of course, the guys in my cell were all short-timers, their crimes being largely misdemeanors while my charges were felonies. A lot of them figured I was a heavy duty criminal, considering my charges.

I quickly learned God was going to use even this for His purposes. By now, whenever someone began asking me what happened to me, it became my second nature to use this as an opportunity to tell them what God had done and was doing in my life. And since God knew He had someone who didn't mind telling others about Him, He made full use of this opportunity.

Most of the inmates were in the cell for only a few days, and then they'd go to court before being released or sent to prison. A lot of them, especially the first-timers, were ripe for the pickin'. What I mean is the Holy Spirit had already begun dealing with a lot of them, so they were ready to receive Christ and hungry to know more about God.

Since there were no regular church services held in the jail, on Sunday afternoons several of the new Christians would gather 'round my bed to hear me teach the Bible.

Keep in mind that at this time in my life, my knowledge of the Bible was somewhat limited, but I was ready and willing to pass along whatever I had learned. However, I was bothered that some of the guys who didn't seem to be getting serious, and I shared as much during one of John Harber's weekly visits.

"I don't understand it, John. Some of the guys receive the Lord and immediately get serious about Him. Others receive Him but there doesn't seem to be any change in their lives."

Smiling, as usual, John encouraged me with the following: "Now, Philip, let God worry about that. The Bible reminds us that one person plants a seed, another comes along and waters it, but it is God—and only God—who gives the increase.[8]

"I know it hurts you to see some of the men act as if they're playing games and others when they're led astray by their cellmates. But this is going to happen. We must also keep in mind that not everyone is going to make it to Heaven. Why, even some whom we think will surely make heaven are not going to make it. It's a narrow road and few there be that find it!

"So, keeping this in mind, let God be their judge, and we'll just pray for them, and be an example of Christ's love," added John.

I was learning that while humans tend to "judge a book by its cover," God's ways are so much higher than ours.

First Samuel 16:7 reminds us, "For God looks at the heart, not the outward appearance." It was going to be difficult but I was determined to "practice" looking for the good in others and doing my best to ignore their faults just as, I hoped, they'd overlook mine.

Even the psalmist David was described as "a man with a heart after God" despite moral failures including murder and adultery. But what made David different from others was that "David was quick to repent" and did not walk in darkness as a lifestyle.✝

✝

We're often reminded that God promises to give us the desires of our hearts. This is true. It is important to realize, however, that our hearts and minds must first begin to line up with *His* heart and mind. When this happens we begin to ask God according to what He places in our hearts, which are routinely our "needs" instead of our "wants." It so pleases our heavenly Father to do good things and give good gifts to His children who are walking in obedience and who are totally surrendered to His divine orchestration of their lives!

The old television show, entitled "Father Knows Best" tells it perfectly. 2 Chronicles 16:9 reminds us "the eyes of the Lord move to and fro throughout all the earth that He may strongly support those whose heart is completely His."

May I ask you ... have you reached a place of full surrender? Are you *completely* God's? Or are you holding back something you don't want to surrender? Ask our Lord to search your heart and reveal any area of your life that displeases Him.

There is no coincidence in God—He is all-powerful, all-present and all-knowing, and He is patiently waiting for you to let go completely so that He can pour upon you blessings you cannot contain.✝

CHAPTER 11

FAVOR FROM ABOVE

Ordinarily, visitors were not allowed in the cells, and no one was allowed "contact" visits. Inmates were allowed visitors only on the weekends, but even those visits were conducted over a phone hookup, with your visitor looking at you through a window.

But as my faith grew, I began to realize that mine was certainly no normal case—neither was anyone else's who got serious about the Lord. In other words, I came to the realization that God takes good care of His own, no matter where they are or what their situation.

For example, in addition to John Harber's regular visits, two more Christian brothers began stopping by on the weekends. Representing an organization called the Navigators, Charlie Heinline and Ron Toporoff played a major role in encouraging me, and others, with memorizing scripture. Then there was Danny, a schoolteacher who worked at the jail full-time, preparing men to take the GED. I soon discovered that Danny was also a brother in Christ! And, of course, there was Mr. Rex, a guard who worked the evening shift. Mr. Rex made regular visits to encourage me.

Following one of Mr. Rex's visits, a young Christian inmate asked me, "Hey man, I dig where you're comin' from as far as being real with God, but why are you always talkin' to that hack? Don't you know that if people see you talkin' to a hack in the joint, they're gonna think you're a snitch?"

"I'm getting to the point where it doesn't matter what people think," I responded. "I mean, people are gonna think what they want, no matter what. And as far as talkin' to the hack, well, that man is a human being, just like you and me. And it doesn't matter what kind of uniform he wears down here on earth. God looks at me, you, and him, and sees past all that. And we need to learn to do the same."

Early one morning, I was shocked to see Frederick Kaufman walk into my cell. He was the attorney hired by Joanne who had encouraged me to tell the truth. I later learned that he, too, was on fire for God.

"Hello, Philip," he greeted me with an outstretched hand.

"Why, hello Mr. Kaufman! How in the world did you get in here?" I asked.

"Well, let's just say that God has appointed me as your personal counsel—which I am, providing you continue to follow my suggestions," Mr. Kaufman said. "I was driving down the street, and the Holy Spirit directed me to stop and visit you, so, here I am."[9]

"Well, I'm glad to see you, for more reasons than one. What do you think about this?" I handed him the list of things that the County had improperly done.

"What's this?" he asked.

"One of the inmates suggested that I try to make a deal, and threaten to sue ... "

"Philip," the attorney interrupted, looking me straight in the eye. "'Vengeance is mine; I will repay,' saith the Lord."[10]

He didn't have to say another word. I got the message, loud and clear. In fact, after he left, I tore up the list and chucked it.

My unofficial visitors' list continued to grow. One afternoon I heard a loud "Praise the Lord! Alleluia! Glory to God!" The voice got louder and louder and came nearer and nearer.

In walked Brother Butch, the friend of John Harber's who used to visit me in the hospital. Butch was the wild and crazy guy who some of the patients had labeled a real "Jesus freak." He was a former Miami police officer who turned to crime, got busted, and years later became a Christian. I had never seen him when he wasn't full of joy.

After giving me a big bear hug, Butch began excitedly sharing about a young man who'd just received Jesus as Savior two cells away from ours. He then began walking around my cell, talking to just about every guy in there. One of the trustees told me later that Butch had stopped to talk to guys at just about every cell on our hallway.

After awhile, the sergeant who was always so sarcastic about religion walked in.

"Your time is up! You have to leave now," he spoke harshly.

His attitude didn't seem to bother Butch, who politely thanked him for allowing him to visit.

Later, the sergeant was overheard telling Mr. Rex, "That guy stayed for over three hours, and it will be his last visit at the Broward County Jail!"

It's a good thing he didn't know what the future would bring—he would have to eat those words! A few weeks later, I looked up one morning and was shocked to see Brother Butch walk into my cell. "But I thought you weren't allowed to come back in here because you weren't a licensed minister!" I exclaimed. I later learned that the jail secretary had asked Butch to bring his ministerial identification with him the next time he came for a visit.

"Praise the Lord, Brother. With God all things are possible!" proclaimed Brother Butch. "After the secretary asked for my ID, I felt led to write a letter to my former pastor and tell him what happened. Soon after, I left on vacation to visit my daughter in Louisiana. When I returned, there in my mailbox was a letter from the American Evangelism Association. They had ordained me as a licensed Evangelist! I brought it up here, and they had to let me in! Glory to God!"

"Man, that is fantastic!" I responded.

Throughout the Bible—from Noah to Jesus to disciples—we find references to God promising "favor" to His children. Some of these promises are as follows:

"But Noah found favor in the eyes of the Lord" (Genesis 6:8).

"And let the favor of the Lord our God be upon us and do confirm for us the work of our hands" (Psalms 90:17).

"For he who finds me finds life, and obtains favor from the Lord" (Proverbs 8:35).

"A good man will obtain favor from the Lord, But He will condemn a man who devises evil" (Proverbs 12:2).

"Good understanding produces favor, But the way of the treacherous is hard" (Proverbs 13:15).

"He who finds a wife finds a good thing, and obtains favor from the Lord" (Proverbs 18:22).

"And Jesus kept increasing in wisdom and stature, and in favor with God and man" (Luke 2:52).

Our heavenly Father is not a respecter of persons, and desires ALL of His children to walk in favor! I encourage you to join me in growing in wisdom and stature that we will enjoy favor with both God and man.✝

CHAPTER 12

GOD-INCIDENCES

I had always been an active person, and even the body cast could not hold me down. In fact, whenever my trusty helpers would change my bed sheets, I did what I could to make it easy for them.

Normally, a person in a cast such as mine is supposed to grab the bed rail and pull himself over on his side, enabling the attendant to tuck the old sheet under him, leaving at least half of the new sheet on the mattress. Then, he'd have to flip over to the opposite rail, so the job could be completed on the other side.

That's the *normal* procedure. But before long, I began grabbing hold of the single bar that extended the length of the bed overhead; using my upper body strength, I'd pull my entire body—cast and all—straight up, then swing over onto the top bunk next to my bed. After awhile this got fairly easy, and I sure enjoyed the exercise.

As summer approached, it began to get really warm in our cell, especially with no fans or air conditioning. With the heat, my cast became extra sticky and uncomfortable, causing me to itch something terrible.

On one occasion, Mr. Rex noticed me sticking a pencil under my cast, trying to scratch. The next day he returned with a small gift, which at the time was worth at least a million bucks to me!

"Here," he said, as he handed me one of those long, plastic back scratchers with a little hand on the end. "Maybe this will get the job done."

"Wow," I said, as I carefully moved the handle back and forth beneath my cast, "this is super!"

Much to our surprise, when I pulled out the little hand, it brought with it a big patch of dead skin. By this time, a crowd had gathered around my bed, closely watching this minor surgery.

To be honest, it had been a couple of days since I'd had this many people who were brave enough to come this close to me. You see, the jail menu included a lot of starchy foods, including beans with every meal. And since getting on the bedpan was so embarrassing and a real hassle to my helper, I waited as long as possible before mounting my throne. Because of this, I usually had enough gas to heat one's home for an entire winter. I don't think it was my imagination that some guys would even volunteer for extra work detail just so they could stay away from our cell.

As time went by I reached the point that nothing surprised me. Time and time again things happened for my benefit that I would call coincidental. But as Sister Phoebe used to say, it was "God-incidental."

For example, I began to make telephone calls from my cell. The telephones were brought around to the cells at different intervals throughout the day and evening. The problem was, the cords weren't long enough to reach way back to me. Even by pushing my bed up to the front of the cell, I still couldn't reach the telephone.

One day Officer Rex walked into our cell carrying a phone attached to a 30-foot cord.

"Here," he said. "I stopped by the phone company on the way to work and picked up an extension cord. Didn't think it was fair, everybody getting to call their honeys 'cept you."

Then there was the miracle of the tape player. For almost two months friends had tried to obtain permission for me to have a tape player so I could listen to preaching and teaching tapes that various churches wanted to donate. By this time I knew Baptists, Methodists, Presbyterians, and folks from various Pentecostal churches. I was able to constantly listen to teaching tapes while in the hospital. Some of my favorite messages were preached by the senior pastor of Ft. Lauderdale's First Baptist Church, O.S. Hawkins. He had such a gift for making the Word so easy to understand! I also really enjoyed the ministry of D. James Kennedy of Coral Ridge Presbyterian. During this time, I learned that many in the Body of Christ insist on being fed only by ministry from their particular denomination. Thankfully, I never believed in denominational divisions—my soul was so hungry for the Word of God that God anointed seemingly every message I heard! I was encouraged by the fact that if God chose to speak to Balaam through a donkey in Numbers 22:28-30, God can surely speak through whatever human He chooses, despite their denomination!

Since moving to the County Jail, my friends tried everything—telephone calls, letters, and even coming to the jail—in an attempt to get permission for a tape player. But it was a no-go.

Once John Harber, Brother Butch, and a local preacher met with the head of the Broward County Jail, just to try to persuade him to approve this simple request. But once again their efforts failed.

One of their excuses was that a tape player would be a security risk; it could be used as a weapon or somebody could harm himself with it. This had to be a cop-out if ever there was one. Even Jim Nolan, president of the Outlaws motorcycle gang, had a guitar in the next cell. If anything could be used as a weapon, a guitar definitely could. The strings could be tied together and used by someone to hang themselves..

Rumor had it the officials were afraid people would record tapes and then smuggle or mail them out to the streets. Tapes of what, I don't know.

I had about given up. But the day after John and company visited the captain's office, Brother Butch came by to visit and describe their final attempt to get me that tape player.

As we were talking, in walked the GED schoolteacher, Danny Radison, who said, "I was praying for you Philip, and afterwards I had the strongest impression that I should bring this to you." He reached into a wrinkled old grocery sack and pulled out a tape player.

I immediately looked at Butch, and we both grinned before simultaneously shouting "Praise the Lord!" And while the player would work fine with batteries, I quickly learned that God wanted me to have the best and not have to keep replacing batteries.

After saying good-bye, Butch and Danny were about to walk out of the cell when they stopped. Butch yelled back at me, saying, "Philly, we'll just have to believe that God will provide electricity so you can hear all the tapes you want."

"He's gonna handle that, too!" I shouted back.

No sooner had I shouted those words, when in walked the head trusty, Stanley Mayes, who excitedly informed us, "Hey! The electricians just pulled up outside. They're here to hook up an electrical outlet for you!"

After that, everybody began shouting, even some of the unbelievers! And sure enough, the electricians installed an outlet—right next to my bed.

That night, Spanky, my new helper, said, "Man, somebody up there must like you, 'cause he sure is takin' care of you."

"Naw, Spanky, it ain't 'somebody,' it's 'someone.' His name is God."

Shaking his head in continued disbelief, Spanky continued, "Man, I've been down four times already, spent every stretch of it right here in the County Jail, and I ain't never heard of 'em putting an electrical socket inside a jail cell. Man, a person could 'lectrocute themselves or start a fire easy. It just don't make sense."

"Well, Spanky," I said, "I'm beginning to realize that there's a whole lotta things that God's behind that don't make sense. But then again, some things we're just not supposed to be able to explain or understand. I guess that's where faith comes in. And just like everybody's runnin' around for almost two months, trying to get me this tape player. Sure looks to me like God was just waitin' on everybody to settle down, get out of the way, and trust in Him to make it happen."

An older trusty, who'd been asleep on his bunk next to us, then rolled over and said, "It's called 'let go, and let God.' Now, would you guys knock it off, so a fella can git his beauty sleep?"

A couple of days later I had an accident that had to be a first: While scratching my itching leg with my back scratcher, it broke! And when I pulled it out of my cast, the little hand was missing; it was still in my cast! I probably could've handled this all right, but because I moved around so much, the tiny plastic fingers began to claw into my leg. Boy, did that smart! After a few days of this, they decided to transport me to the emergency room back at the hospital.

Once again, I was in for a real surprise. Considering my being moved was supposed to be a secret, when I was wheeled into the emergency room, there was John Harber and his pastor.

"Well hello!" they shouted, their voices filled with excitement.

"We've got a real special surprise for you," said Pastor Joe, as he placed a box on my bed.

"What now?" I questioned.

"Well, Philip," said John, "we figured it's about time you were given the opportunity to partake of Holy Communion, so we obtained special permission to serve it to you."

John then turned to the officer who was assigned to stay with me, saying "Would you like to join us in celebrating the Lord's Supper?"

My armed escort said, "Er, well, thank you but, uh, I'm Jewish and ..."

"Well, we certainly don't mind, as long as you're comfortable; after all, Jesus was Jewish, too," said Pastor Joe.

"So he was, so he was ... sure, I'll join you," said Officer Raymond. And we all joined hands to pray.

To say the least, I'll never forget that first time to take communion—well, the first time to take communion and mean what I was doing! Sure, I had gone through the motions of it time and time again while growing up in church, but it never really meant very much.

This time, however, I had my heart right, so it wasn't a ritual—it proved to be a very moving experience.

After communion, the orthopedic doctor came in with a real weird-looking electric saw in his hand. "Let's have a look at your cast," he said, pulling the sheet away.

"Praise God," I shouted.

"Now, about where are you experiencing the most discomfort?" asked the doctor.

"About right here, Doc," I responded. I watched him mark the spot with a pencil. He then plugged in his saw and flipped the switch.

"Are you sure that's not gonna cut my leg, Doc?" I asked, as sawdust flew into the air.

"No, no," he laughed. "Here, watch this," and he touched the spinning blade against my arm.

I stared at the blade, which wasn't cutting my skin. "I can't believe it," I said.

"The blade doesn't actually spin, it vibrates," he explained, "and this causes the blade to cut into the cast."

"Well I'll be," I whispered, as I watched him complete a tiny square around the mark he'd made on the cast. When he popped the little window out of the cast, we all looked inside and began laughing, for he had certainly hit pay dirt!

There was the plastic hand, which the doctor then removed with a small pair of forceps. And, oh, what a relief that was!

"Why look, Phil, God isn't the only one who has his hand on you!" John joked.

"You have some nasty cracks in your cast. I'm going to admit you for a couple of days to make some repairs," said the doctor.

"Suits me," I grinned.

"I didn't think you'd mind," he grinned back at me.

I know he knew I wouldn't mind at all, because the hospital was like the Hilton compared to the County Jail!

That night it was like old home week, as I was reunited with my old hospital friends, plus a roomful of Christian friends from various churches.

After the reunion ended and all my visitors left, I found myself in an empty hospital room. As I began to drift off to sleep I smiled as I was reminded of just how much my Christian family had grown since the night I received Jesus as Savior only a few months ago. Indeed, God means business when He promises we will inherit "mothers and fathers, sisters and brothers" when we join His family!

That night I enjoyed the most restful sleep I could remember.

We're often reminded that God promises to give us the desires of our hearts. This is true. It is important to realize, however, that our hearts and minds must first begin to line up with heart and mind. When this happens we begin to ask God according to what He places in our hearts, which are routinely our "needs" instead of our "wants." It so pleases our heavenly Father to do good things and give good gifts to His children who are walking in obedience and who are totally surrendered to His divine orchestration of their lives!

The old television show, entitled "Father Knows Best" tells it perfectly. 2 Chronicles 16:9 reminds us "the eyes of the Lord move to and fro throughout all the earth that He may strongly support those whose heart is completely His."

May I ask you ... have you reached a place of full surrender? Are you God's? Or are you holding back something you don't want to surrender? Ask our Lord to search your heart and reveal any area of your life that displeases Him.

There is no coincidence in God—He is all-powerful, all-present and all-knowing, and He is patiently waiting for you to let go completely so that He can pour upon you blessings you cannot contain.

CHAPTER 13

TRIALS

Our cell's window stretched the entire length of one wall, high up near the ceiling. Though the cobwebs also stretched from wall to wall and the pane was coated with a layer of thick dust, I could still see that April showers had arrived. In fact, I could also feel the rain, as a steady drip created a puddle next to my bed.

I had been looking forward to this month, not because of the rain, but because it was time to go to trial, and I was ready!

Under normal circumstances most people would probably dread going to court, especially if one faced the penalties that I could receive. Needless to say, my situation was definitely not the norm.

First of all, I knew that until I went to trial, I was not going to get out of this cast and begin walking again. It wasn't that I had gotten tired of bedpans and beans. I had learned to live with these.

Most importantly, I was eager to find out what God was going to do next; deep down, I knew it would be good.

Months before, a local Presbyterian preacher named Bob Koren had given me a scriptural promise, which he said was already in effect for my life. His exact words were, "Philip, Romans 8:28 says 'and we know that all things work together for good to them that love God, to them who are the called according to his purpose.'"

Time and time again those words came to mind, especially when I experienced God working miraculously on my behalf, turning negatives into positives.

Because of this, I was excitedly looking forward to the outcome of my trial. In other words, regarding this Christianity stuff, I hadn't just found the key to abundant life—I had "really found it!" Thus, the T-shirt I wore during my three-day trial became very special to me.

"Here, put this on," said John Harber, the day before going to court. "Phoebe asked me to give this to you. She knew you'd wear it proudly," he added.

It was gold-colored shirt, with the words "I Really Found It" emblazoned across the front. I could not have guessed that these words would soon be featured on the front pages of local newspapers, as well as on the nightly news.

✝ ✝ ✝

As I was wheeled down the hallway of the County Jail that morning, you should have heard the applause, jeers, and support.

"Take it to the wire, Christian!"

"Keep the Faith, Philip!"

And even, "Give 'em hell, turkey!"

I was grinning from ear to ear, but most importantly, I was grinning on the inside. For once in my life, a peace was flowing through me, sort of like a river flowing over and over. But I wasn't gonna "give 'em hell," I was gonna "give 'em heaven!"

✝ ✝ ✝

Even the courthouse hallway was lined with people as the medics pushed my stretcher toward the courtroom. Sure, the curiosity seekers were there because they'd heard about my case on the 10:00 P.M. news or had read about it in the newspaper. But even they were outnumbered, as Christian supporters from seemingly every church in Fort Lauderdale were on hand to stand by me, just as they'd done for the previous seven months.

As I was about to enter the courtroom, I recognized a face that I hadn't seen in many months. It belonged to John Apostolou, the man who'd put the .357 magnum to my head.

But this time, my mind was not filled with fear and paranoia. I smiled at him and said, "God loves you very much."

If looks could kill, his response to my statement should've left me six feet under. Not surprisingly, I even expected it, although I meant exactly what I had said to him.

I was taken all the way to the front of the courtroom, where a rented hospital bed awaited me. Had I known that I would repeat this process three consecutive days while the trial dragged on longer than even the prosecutor expected, my enthusiasm would have lessened.

Actually, Broward County Prosecutor Brian Kay came close to having a much weaker case than anticipated. Despite my charges of midnight burglary, attempted murder, and possession of a burglary tool, my public defender discovered that John Apostolou told the State that he didn't want to prosecute. He told them he wanted to drop the charges against me.

Also, when my public defender ran a check on him, he discovered that my attacker had a long list of arrests, including charges such as assault on a police officer and weapons charges—yet he was always acquitted. We definitely smelled a snitch, or someone who was working both sides of the fence. But with no convictions, information such as this could not be included in our defense.

When the smoke cleared, the state had somehow talked John into prosecuting.

Finally, court was in session.

The first three rows on one side of the room were filled with young people. One of the first things my judge did was recognize this group, which was visiting from a local junior high school. They were using their field trip to learn what takes place in a court of law during a trial, and I was the object of their lesson. Judge Price took time to introduce them to the court reporter, bailiff, prosecutor, public defender, and me.

I just smiled and waved at them. They probably thought I was going off the deep end.

During the first recess, I looked across the wooden railing that separated me from the visitors and was surprised to see John Harber and Brother Butch talking to a fellow who looked strangely familiar. He turned out to be the criminal attorney who had been hired by my fall partner, Tom, to defend me—the one who had told me to get word to Tom that he needed $10,000 before he'd even consider taking on my case. When he came back to see if I'd gotten the bread, which I hadn't, I told him that I'd become a Christian.

While I didn't know it at that time, this attorney was a member of a local church, and he immediately figured that I had "jailhouse religion." This is what they call a person who gets into trouble then suddenly becomes religious, hoping to get a lighter sentence.

It turned out the guy belonged to the church attended by some of my friends, and he had been kept informed of my situation during the previous seven months. He had come to the courtroom with the following message for me, which he passed along via my public defender.

"Listen Philip," said my P.D., "this attorney says he's sorry he doubted you before, and now he even believes in you. However, he's suggesting that whatever you do, don't bring up the Lord's name in the courtroom, because there have been so many defendants who've done this who've only been playing games. He feels that it will only make it worse on you."

"Tell him I appreciate his concern," I said, "but a man's gotta do what he's gotta do."

"Does this mean you're still going to take the stand?" he asked.

"Yes, because the Holy Spirit is directing me to tell the truth, even if doing so further incriminates me," I responded.

"Philip," he continued, "everything is going to be stacked against you. You were caught red-handed in the apartment, you gave them a recorded confession, the guy who shot you and the arresting officers are going to testify; you have everything to lose and nothing to gain by taking the stand."

"Listen Michael," I said, "I know where you're coming from, and I do appreciate everything you've done for me. But let's face it. You and I both know I'm going to be found guilty anyway. So what's it going to hurt if I tell my side? Even if it means telling the jury why I now have to tell the truth—because of my conversion to Christianity?"

"Well, have it your way, and I wish you luck," he said.

✞ ✞ ✞

During the second day of the trial, I couldn't help but notice a young girl who was sitting in the second row, next to the aisle. She stared intently at me the entire morning. In fact, she seemed to be ignoring all the proceedings. Instead, she just kept staring at me.

Later that day, I found out why.

"Her name is Laura," said John Harber during a lunchtime visit. "She was here with her class yesterday, but she received special permission from both her parents and her teacher to return today. She told me she just could not believe that you could look so peaceful lying up there in your body cast, with all these people saying all these terrible things about you, and facing life in prison ... and yet you're so at peace you actually look like you are asleep. She said she just had to come back and see you again."

"Well, John," I interrupted, "I'll bet I know what you told her."

"You betcha. I was able to tell her all about how Christ has given you a new lease on life, and it is the peace and joy of the Holy Spirit that she sees all over you."

"Isn't that great!?" I asked.

"Yes it is, Brother," John continued. "Second Corinthians 3:2 points out that Christians are 'living epistles, known and read of all men.' Just like Laura was watching you, people are watching Christians everywhere to find out if they're real or not, to see how they respond during rough times. This is what wins people to Christ, when they see there really is something to this Christianity. Then they, too, will want this for their lives."

✝ ✝ ✝

Finally, the day arrived that I had been patiently awaiting. I would get the opportunity to tell my side of the story.

Naturally, I couldn't take the stand, so they pushed my hospital bed over to a spot right in front of the jury.

I then began to tell the whole truth, and for the first time in my life, nothing but the truth, so help me God. I didn't leave out a single detail.

While my admission of guilt probably looked real foolish, I did notice several of the jurors seemed to take a real interest in my version. And when I finished, the judge immediately sent the jury in to deliberate.

Much to the surprise of the judge, prosecutor, and my public defender, the jury didn't return with a quick verdict. In fact, we waited one hour...then two hours ... then three hours ... and finally, the jury returned.

"Your Honor," said the head juror, "we'd like a clarification on an issue. Regarding the charge of attempted murder, if we don't feel that the defendant is guilty of this charge, can it be dropped?"

"Well," responded the judge, "you can find the defendant guilty of a lesser charge, say, second degree attempt, meaning he was an accomplice, but not guilty of actual attempt."

"Then that is what we want to do, Your Honor," continued the juror. "We, the jury, find the defendant guilty of midnight burglary, second degree attempt, and possession of burglary tools."

"I then order a pre-sentence investigation to be done on Mr. Hicks' behalf, and hereby schedule sentencing for June 15, 1979," stated Judge Price before rising to leave.

Throughout my hospitalization and trial, it was amazing that I was now in a "fishbowl" and people were constantly watching to see how I would respond, just as the young student named Laura had returned to court because she found it so difficult to believe that a person could remain at peace in the midst of such a storm.

Because I had sought the Lord and begun to anchor my life in Him, His grace was constantly proving my source of strength regardless the challenges of each day.

I encourage you to "seek the Lord" now while all is well, so that your heart and soul will be prepared when adversity comes your way.✝

CHAPTER 14

LETTERS

Five weeks had passed since my trial and, quite frankly, I was looking forward to my day of sentencing. Meanwhile, I kept busy.

Following the trial, a man came to see me who asked me question after question regarding my past. He planned to use these to compile a report on my past life, which the judge would consider before sentencing me.

Also, my public defender asked me to write everyone I knew who I thought might write a positive letter of reference on my behalf. I just didn't feel good about doing this, and during a visit with John Harber, I brought up this subject.

"I just don't feel right about asking all these people to write letters for me," I told John. "Although a lot of them are respected citizens, including lawyers and various types of businessmen, the majority of them are not Christians. I partied with them, drank with them, did drugs with them. I just don't feel right about it."

"You've got to follow your heart," said John, "and God will certainly honor your decision."

In the end, I only asked people to write letters who I knew were Christians, including those who were acquainted with both me and my parents.

✞ ✞ ✞

By this time I was receiving so much correspondence that I didn't even have time to answer it all. In addition, my tape library was growing at a rapid pace. In fact, I had received teaching tapes from so many different churches that I could listen to only a few.

Nobody could ever say that I wasn't given plenty of opportunity to grow spiritually, and I was taking advantage of every opportunity.

As I was to find out later, it's a good thing I did.

In Genesis 50:20 we read, "But as for you, you meant evil against me; but God meant it for good, in order to bring about as it is this day, to save many people alive."

While the sergeant thought he would have the last laugh, it is God who revels in demonstrating that He alone is sovereign, and no one can close a door that He desires to be open.

Brother Butch kept a good attitude toward the sergeant and held no animosity toward him, and meanwhile, God was at work orchestrating the steps and actions necessary to open wide the jail "to save many people."✞

CHAPTER 15

SENTENCING

June 15, 1979 finally arrived, and as crazy as it might sound, I was excited! Today I would find out what tomorrow would bring; at least as far as the court was concerned.

Once again the courtroom was packed as they wheeled me down the center aisle. It looked like half the city was there, including photographers and reporters from every local newspaper, radio, and television station!

There was the Major from the County Jail, along with the Lieutenant who'd been personally assigned to my case.

And the Christians! They must've come out of the walls!

"Howdy, Michael!" I greeted my public defender as he approached my bed.

Shaking my outstretched hand, Michael spoke in his always serious manner, "I do wish you the best Philip. You certainly have been an inspiration to me. I just wish I could have done more to help you."

Interrupting, I said, "Now listen, don't start that again. I thought you did a wonderful job, considering everything was stacked against us!"

"Please rise," came a voice from the front of the courtroom, as Judge Price entered from his chambers.

"Mr. Hicks, before pronouncing sentence, do you have anything to say?" asked Judge Price.

Hesitating briefly I calmly replied, "Your Honor I just want you to know that I am very sorry that I did what I did, and I do regret causing anyone any pain and anguish that they've experienced. Also, regardless of what happens here today, I don't and won't blame anybody but myself, for I now realize that a man must reap whatever he sows."

From somewhere in the back of the courtroom I heard an "Amen," then someone laughed.

"Well, Mr. Hicks," said Judge Price, "after reading your pre-sentence investigation I can safely say that I have never read so many letters from such a diverse background as those that were written in your behalf. Letters were written by doctors, lawyers, a state senator, a sheriff, ministers, and from people all over the United States. Why, you even had a letter written on your behalf from across the ocean—from England! And not a single negative word about you! This has made my job most difficult."

For the first time, I began to feel uneasy.

"And yet, while I read all the positive, I must still remind myself of these most serious crimes of which you have been convicted. While I don't doubt the change that has taken place in your life, today I must sentence the old Philip Hicks. Therefore, I sentence you to a consecutive sentence of life plus thirty plus five years, and I want you to serve a mandatory three years on both Counts one and two."

Continuing, the judge explained, "The life sentence is for count one, which is midnight burglary; thirty years is for count two, attempted murder; and the remaining five years is for count three, possession of burglary tools."

"Your Honor, I object," interjected my public defender. "Defendant was found guilty of second degree attempt, which carries a maximum sentence of fifteen years, and you have given him thirty!"

"Hmmm, so I have, Counselor," responded the judge. "Well, in that case," I'll subtract even five more years from that and we'll make it life plus ten plus five."

The courtroom was silent. No doubt several in attendance felt the sentence would be much more lenient. In fact, since it was my first offense, some even expected me to get probation. I thought to myself—on paper it may be my first offense, but in reality it was my first time caught! I had spent twenty-nine years sowing bad seed, and sooner or later one must reap what he sows.[11]

Deep in my heart, I had already known that I would definitely spend some time in prison. I also knew it wouldn't be for long—yet long enough to come to terms with God for the first time in my life.

After all, I had been walking with the devil for close to twenty-nine years, and it would take quite some time to get established in my new faith. As deep as I was in sin, it would've been far too easy for me to slide right back into my old way of life, and of course God knew this.

"Judge Price, Judge Price," I called out, as he was about to exit the courtroom. When he turned back around I said, "I just want to thank you. I think you're a good judge, and you had to do what you had to do."

"Thank you, Mr. Hicks, and I hope you continue with God."

I turned to my public defender and said, "Michael, I want to speak to my prosecutor."

Overhearing this, my prosecutor said, "What is it you want?"

"Sir, I just want you to know that I had never before seen a trial, and I thought you did a heck of a job!"

He seemed startled by my compliment, but nevertheless he said, "Er, thank you, Mr. Hicks," before he quickly walked away.

And then I was surrounded!

In tears, my precious sister Phoebe hugged me and said, "Philip, this card is for you. It has been signed by over thirty of your brothers and sisters who are here today to support you."

Then about thirty people were hugging and kissing me all at once.

"I believe we should pray, and I would like to lead us, OK, Phoebe?" I asked.

"Oh Philip, this is just like you. Of course," she said.

After everyone surrounded my bed and joined hands, I began.

"Dear God, we all know who is in control of our lives, and for this realization we are most thankful. We thank You for Your love and mercy and Your wonderful Holy Spirit, which even now unites us as one, in a family of love.

"Your Word reminds us that it is Your will for us to 'give thanks in all circumstances,' yes, even when we don't quite feel like it.

"Nevertheless, today we obediently offer up a sacrifice of praise to You, giving thanks even for this prison sentence, and for everything that You have planned for each of us.

"We especially thank You for all the seeds that You have sown through us during this trial, and would ask that You continue to use us to encourage others by the Word of our testimonies.

"In Jesus' name we pray, Amen."

✞ ✞ ✞

Back at the county jail later that evening, once again I was surrounded.

"Man, I thought you got screwed!" said a young inmate who'd recently received Christ. "I mean, how could they do that to you? Why, you could've murdered somebody and got off lighter. It just ain't fair."

"Now, now," I said, "it doesn't make any difference what kind of sentence they gave me. I know I'm not going to have to do much time. I've seen God work over and over in my life, and He's gonna work again, but all in His own perfect time. After all, we must remind ourselves that He knows what's best for us, and we're on His timetable now, not ours. And while I appreciate your thinking my sentence isn't fair, let's be reminded of our Lord Jesus, and what they did to Him. Despite His innocence, they tortured and crucified Him. If ever there was anyone who was treated unfairly, it was Him and only Him! And how did He respond to the injustice? He prayed and said, 'Father, forgive them for they know not what they do.' I'm guilty. He wasn't. And I deserve whatever sentence given me. He didn't."

About that time, Officer Rex walked into the cell, smiled, and said, "Hey, why don't you guys give Hicks a breather? Anyway, he probably wants to call his sweetie, don't you Hicks?"

"Hey, yeah. It's already nine o"clock, Colorado time, and she's off work," I quickly responded. "Thanks, Mr. Rex, good lookin' out!"

In a matter of moments I had broken the news to Joyce, who was freaking out on the other end of the line.

"Now sweetheart," I consoled her, "it'll be all right. Just you wait and see. Why, I won't do more than three years, and I'll be out of here!"

At that time of my life, I had not yet learned how much power there is in the spoken word. In due time I was to find out.

Nevertheless, that night I wrote Joyce a long letter. Since I didn't know how long I'd be incarcerated, I knew I couldn't ask her to wait for me. So as difficult as it was, I had to let her go, and she had to let me go.

So very much had occurred in the nine months since joining God's family. After being knocked down, I found myself all alone—with no family nearby, no money, literally

no clothes (except a hospital gown), and my life was a miserable wreck! And then, nine months later, more than thirty Christians stood by me to face what could have been the most devastating day of my life! No, I wasn't alone anymore, and the peace that filled my soul was beyond comprehension! I *knew* that I could look toward tomorrow with confidence that once again My Father in heaven would prove Himself faithful! I was enjoying such a sweet peace that surpassed all understanding.✝

CHAPTER 16

THE MIDDLE OF THE DESERT

It was barely dawn the next morning when I felt a tap on my shoulder. I looked up to find Officer Rex smiling down at me.

"Hey, what are you still doing here?" I asked. "You usually leave at midnight, don't you?"

"Fella, I've already gone home and come back. The captain said he needed a man to accompany you on your flight, and here I am. Hope you don't mind," he said, with a wink.

"Aw man, I thought I didn't have to see your ugly face again," I answered, as I dodged his attempt to punch me.

Two hours later we arrived at what looked like a private airport. "Hope you appreciate the trouble they've gone through for you," joked Officer Rex as he helped lift me into the airplane. "Why, they had to charter a private plane... just for you!"

"Yeah," I said, "and don't tell me you're the stewardess!"

Since I had to lie flat on my back while riding in the airplane, all I could see was clouds.

But that didn't matter; I was fairly preoccupied as my mind flashed back over the past 10 months. It was hard to believe that I would soon be out of my temporary plaster home.

My thoughts were interrupted by Officer Rex, who said, "Buckle your seat belt. We're about to land. Oh, you don't have a seat belt, do you?" This time he had to dodge my hand.

Thirty minutes later I was choked up inside as I had to say good-bye to still another Christian friend, Mr. Rex. Even though he wore a uniform, I had grown to love and respect this man and was very thankful that God had assigned him his position at the Broward County Jail.

✞ ✞ ✞

As a norm, when inmates arrive at the Lake Butler, Florida, Reception and Medical Center, they are told to strip down, leave their belongings in a pile, and hit the shower. They then exit the showers via a different room, where they spend several hours while being processed.

But, of course, my situation was definitely not the norm.

"Hey, sarge, would you look at this," yelled an officer. "Hey, man, did you git hit by a Mack truck? Hope you got his license! Ha! Hey, sarge, how ya s'pose ta strip search dis turkey?"

"Just git his butt up to the hospital ward, and hurry it up!" said a rather mean-looking guy, who had a mouthful of chewing tobacco.

Soon I found myself in a cold, quiet room that looked to be the size of a tennis court. The room was lined with hospital beds against both walls, but I was the only patient.

I immediately felt like I was back in a desert. I turned my head away from the door, wiping a tear as fast as I could, hoping no one had seen me.

If only I could just see one person I know, I thought to myself.

"Hi, pumpkin," said a voice from the doorway, "I'm Mrs. Greer, one of the nurse's aides. Now don't you worry, the rest of the guys are down at the TV room. You can believe you'll have company as soon as they call chow! Here, have a peppermint, sweetie.

As a peace quickly flowed over me, I realized that I was not alone, in more ways than one.

I smiled and said, "Thanks, Mrs. Greer, thank you very much!

✞ ✞ ✞

My dad and I had agreed that my mom shouldn't have to know about my situation until at least after my trial. In fact, he once wrote and suggested that "maybe you'll be given probation, then you can come to Memphis and tell her yourself. But as for now, just write me in care of my office, and we'll keep this a secret."

But of course, we should have known better. After all, mothers have built-in radar. Call it intuition or whatever; they know when something isn't right. And my mom was no exception. The following is an excerpt from a letter written by my mother, which I received shortly after my arrival at Lake Butler:

> Dear Son,
>
> Once again, my heart is broken. I just don't know where I went wrong. Your Dad and I tried our best to raise you three boys in the best way we knew how. I was always so proud when I'd look down from my seat in the church choir, and see you sitting there. I just don't know what I did wrong. Months ago I knew something wasn't right with you; I just couldn't put my finger on it. You kept writing me, telling me all about an "experience" you'd had with God. Yes, I was mighty proud, and yet, something just wasn't right. Plus, your girlfriend, Joyce, addressed every letter, and it was odd that she always wrote a separate letter to us, using the same envelope, postmarked in Aspen. Well, because of God's grace, I'll get by. Your Dad and I are planning a trip to come and visit you.

Hopefully, we can come down there sometime around Christmas.

I love you very much son. Be sweet.

Love, Mother

Days later, I finally got up the nerve to answer her letter, which went as follows:

Dear Mother,

I love you very, very much. Without a doubt, you're the best mother in this entire world. So often I wanted to write and tell you the truth regarding my circumstances. And yet, for once I wanted to honor Pop's suggestion, and we agreed it'd be best this way. I hope I'm able to finish this letter. Already I'm finding it very difficult to express my thoughts. Mother, I'm so very sorry that I've hurt you again. You sure don't deserve all the rough times I've put you through. Before I became a Christian down in Fort Lauderdale, I thought of you often and knew how this would break your heart if and when you found out about it.

Honestly, I wanted to kill myself. But, I guess that would have been the selfish way out...easy for me, but even rougher on you. Mother, you gotta believe this. This is not your fault. You were faithful to raise me up in the church. You can't blame all this on yourself. You did just what the Bible tells parents to do. You trained me up, and after that I had the option to choose my own path.[12] That was my choice. Then again, the Bible also promises that if a parent does train up their children in the way they should go, then when they are old, they'll return to those ways." Ya see Mom, I came back, all because of your raising me right. You didn't give up on me; you kept praying! So, please, please, get rid of all that guilt. It's simply not your fault. In fact, I am confident that it was your prayers that kept me from getting killed the night

> that I was shot, as well as the times I was involved in car wrecks, motorcycle wrecks, and the day the horse flipped over on top of me, after I had flipped over its head while riding! I'm sure looking forward to you and Pop visiting me at Christmas. Thanks for writing. Your letter was the highlight of my week.
>
> Love, Phil

My first three months at Lake Butler proved to be a totally different world from my life as a young Christian back in Fort Lauderdale. Now it seemed so long ago when Christian brothers and sisters almost continually surrounded me.

I longed for fellowship with sincere Christians. Most of the professing believers whom I'd met here in the hospital were using pages from their Bibles for rolling papers, either for tobacco or grass. The latter was being smuggled in by free people who worked here at the hospital, as well as some of the inmates who had been permanently assigned to Lake Butler. And yet, the last thing I would ever do was snitch on them. Oftentimes, I'd remember Brother Butch's sound advice.

"Now Philly, it don't matter how strong a Christian you are, or what your motives are; one of the cardinal sins at the joint is snitching! Don't you ever snitch! Now, there's a big difference between telling the truth, like you were led to do at your trial, and snitching. People snitch to get brownie points and sometimes they'll get away with it. On the other hand, that's the quickest way to get stabbed, and sooner or later a person is gonna get caught!"

I guess the worst part of my "desert experience" was the lack of Christian friends. Even the weekly Bible study turned out to be a bummer because the chaplain didn't seem to care. And since I had always been an outgoing person, I found myself compromising my faith. I'd get caught up in conversations discussing all kinds of subjects, about which I'm certain the

Lord would have been very unhappy. I even started smoking again. Since I smoked only four or five cigarettes a day, it was more out of boredom than habit.

"Hello, my name is Orlando Gonzalez, what's yours?" asked a new patient, who looked like he could easily be playing linebacker for the Chicago Bears.

"Hi, my name is Philip. Where are you from, Orlando?" I asked.

Raising his head proudly, he answered, "I am from Cuba; but I have lived in Miami for almost ten years!"

Orlando then offered me a cigarette, which I accepted, and then he began telling me about his crime.

Although I hadn't been incarcerated long, I had already learned that in the joint guys don't often bring up their crime and the reason for their incarceration. In fact, the vast majority of those behind bars insist they have been framed and they are innocent! So my conversation with Orlando was definitely not the norm, as here were two guys and both of us were admitting we were guilty!

After he finished, I described to him the events that led up to my acceptance of Christ; but somehow my words seemed so shallow, as I spoke between puffs.

Nevertheless we became good friends, and suddenly, life wasn't so lonely any more.

✞ ✞ ✞

The days turned into weeks, and finally my cast was scheduled for removal; my doctors were planning to perform corrective surgery within a week.

Orthopedic technicians carefully removed my cast as my new doctors watched. "Easy does it, that's it, now ... just lower yourself down gently. There, that wasn't so bad, now was it?" asked Dr. Hankins, one of the two orthopedic surgeons who had been assigned to me.

Once again I discovered that God does indeed take excellent care of his children. My case had been personally assigned to the best orthopedic surgeons on staff at Shands Teaching Hospital in nearby Gainesville, Florida. Doctors Dusek and Hankins were known as two of the best in their field. In fact, their patients included the casualties from the Florida Gator football games. They both demonstrated so much care and concern for my well-being.

Not that I would've complained, but since arriving three months before, I'd seen some of the state prison doctors treat their patients fairly poorly. No doubt some of them had been burned more than once by con men who manipulated them to get drugs. I can speak from experience, because I had done the very same thing back in Fort Lauderdale prior to my conversion experience.

"Gosh, Doc," I said, "my leg sure did get skinny, and hey, is that where the bullet went in? Look, the skin's all grown back!"

"Considering it's been almost an entire year since you walked, I'd have to say your leg looks very healthy," responded Dr. Hankins. "They must have fed you well in southern Florida. Did you go jogging on the beach as well?"

We both laughed.

He took hold of my right foot, placed a hand under my knee, and attempted to bend my leg. "Uh-oh," he said, "just what I was afraid of … ossification."

"Hey Doc," I said, "What does that mean? C'mon down to my level. What does ossa-whatever mean?"

"Calcium deposits have built up, causing new bone to form," answered the doctor.

"Well, what's all this mean, Doc?" I asked.

"I'm going to have to postpone surgery for still another week. We'll have to anesthetize you on Saturday and literally snap your leg. If we don't do that, then you'll walk like Chester for the rest of your life," explained the doctor.

I quickly recalled Chester as the deputy to Sheriff Matt Dillon on the popular television western called *Gunsmoke*.

"OK, Doc, anything you say... I sure don't want to walk like Chester, although I do feel like I took part in an episode of *Gunsmoke*! Besides, I've waited over eleven months—the least I can do is wait another week or two," I said.

"You don't plan on going anywhere, do you?" quipped the doctor.

Smiling, I shook my head and said, "Well, the judge said I'd have to bring him life plus fifteen."

✝ ✝ ✝

Saturday morning finally arrived, and my head was already floating. I was on the operating table with an I.V. running some type of clear fluid into my arm. I could hear the conversation nearby, but I couldn't quite make out what was being said.

I looked up and recognized the familiar faces of my two doctors.

"Now this shouldn't hurt a bit, but you will definitely be sore for a while afterwards," warned one of the doctors. He was holding some type of thick object under my knee.

Without warning, one of the doctors brought my right foot straight down, and a crunching sound came from inside my kneecap. It sounded similar to when a dentist once smashed one of my wisdom teeth with a dental tool.

And just like the doctor warned, it didn't hurt a bit—until the next morning.

But I didn't care, for this was yet one more step toward walking. I was determined to never take walking for granted again!

✝

Why was I not surprised when I learned my two doctors also served as the team physicians for the Florida Gators football team and that they had operated on previous winners of the Heisman Trophy? After all, the Lord gave His only Son to die for the salvation of the world, but his giving didn't stop there. Our Father wants His children to have the best of everything, including medical treatment!

Of course this hasn't helped my throwing arm any, but I can dance with the best of them.✝

CHAPTER 17

OLD HABITS

"Felipe! Como esta?"

For a second I thought I was dreaming! Then it dawned on me that I was still at the Lake Butler Hospital, and that finally, after 366 days, I had undergone surgery on my leg.

Then came that voice again. "Felipe! Como esta?"

I opened my eyes, and there on the bed next to mine sat a grinning Orlando. "Man," he said, "you been sleeping since ten o'clock this morning, when you came back from surgery! Man, you gonna sleep your life away? C'mon, let's party, Hermano!"

"Oh-h-h-h-h," I murmured. "I feel like my leg was run over by a train or something. And now I gotta put up with an unemployed comedian!"

"C'mon, man, let's go shoot some hoops," he said, laughing.

I unhooked the blue urinal that hung on the side of my bed and started to throw it at this clown, but I froze because it hurt so badly to turn.

"Hey man, would you call the nurse and tell her I need something for pain," I pleaded.

"Just what I thought. You're fakin' it so you can get a fix!" said Orlando.

This time I reared back and threw the urinal, grimacing in pain as I exclaimed, "Why you!"

"Uno momento, uno momento, Felipe, I'll get the nurse," laughed my retreating friend as he headed out of the room.

✝ ✝ ✝

"Well, Doc, exactly what did you do to my leg?" I asked Dr. Hankins an hour or so later.

"We performed a successful femoral osteotomy on your right femur," he replied. "We removed a portion of bone from your upper right hip and used it to rebuild your badly fractured femur bone," he continued.

"When will I be able to walk again?" I asked.

"Just be patient," he replied, "and we'll try to get you up on crutches in two to three weeks. Try not to rush things, and you'll experience far better results in the long run."

"You're the boss, Doc, you're the boss," I said.

✝ ✝ ✝

It had been over a month since surgery, and I had been moved to two different rooms since then.

"One thing about this place," I said, "they sure fix it so you meet a lot of different people."

"Ain't that the damn truth," said Gene, a real skinny fellow in the next bed who talked with a country accent that was as slow as molasses.

"What on earth happened to you?" I asked Gene, who had both of his legs and one arm in casts and a big bandage on his head. Most of his teeth were also missing.

"Got run over by a car," he answered as he rolled himself a smoke. "Hey, want one?" he asked.

"No thanks, I'm trying to quit," I said.

"Yeah, I had ripped off this nice old pickup truck at a garage near Bartow, and the next week I went back and stole a bunch of tools," he said, "but then, as I wuz runnin' across the highway, this fool ran me over … and here I am, back for my fifth run here at the country club north. They give me a pair of fives, running wild, for grand theft auto, a B&E, and possession of stolen property. The damn judge tried to git me on the habitual o-fender charge, but my lawyer got me off! So, you're the Christian dude I ben hearin' 'bout?" Gene questioned.

"Yeah, guess so," I replied.

"That Bible's all right for sum folks, but not me. Too many contradictions in it," said Gene. "I guarantee ya one thing, when you get to the Rock, you're gonna have to trade that Bible in fer a shank! Them cats don't go fer jailhouse religion, and they's liable to make a sissy outta ya if you try hidin' behin' that religion."

"Each to his own, Gene, but no matter what you or anybody else thinks about me, I'm sticking to my faith. I admit that while I went to church all my life, I wasn't a real Christian. But that's because I never knew the Lord in my heart. I was religious but didn't have a relationship with God. And although I had to get knocked down before I looked up, I don't care what others think. We're all gonna be judged one of these days, and I know in my heart it's real. So for now, I'll let my talk match my walk."

"Don't look to me like you're doin' much walkin'," he replied.

We both laughed.

"You got that right!" I said.

✝ ✝ ✝

A few nights later, "lights out" had already been called, and I was lying in bed thinking when I overheard some conversation nearby. Gene and another inmate were talking about me.

"Yeah, but all the cat ever does is read that Bible and work on them Bible studies the chaplain gives him. And did you ever talk to him? He really knows that Bible, inside and out! I think he's fer real, don't you?" said a muffled voice.

"Man, I dun seen dudes come thru heah totin' dem Bibles, then when they git out, they throw them away," said a voice, which I knew belonged to Gene.

"Yeah, but I knew a guy down at Avon Park that got serious about God. After he got out, he started preachin' on the streets, and now he even goes back into the joint. In fact, Bobby Ray Wallace told me the guy even teaches the Bible in a *church* on the street! And, 'fore he left Avon, a whole bunch of dudes got saved, and I mean to tell you, they's fer real!" answered the unidentified voice.

"Maybe so," said Gene, "but that crap ain't fer me. My old lady crammed that stuff down me all my life, and finally I even left home behind it! So I sure don't have to come to the joint and listen to it!"

What will it take to make people believe in me? I thought to myself as I slowly drifted off to sleep.

✝ ✝ ✝

In the joint, guys make a gadget called a "stinger" which is used to heat their coffee. The Lake Butler Hospital was no exception. To make them, you separate two razor blades with some match sticks, and then bind them together with string. Then, you attach wire to this. When you're ready to heat water, you drop the stinger into the water and stick the wires into the electric socket. In a matter of moments your water is boiling. But the stingers are considered contraband, because a guy could either get shocked or start a fire. And yet it was the only way to heat our water, as coffee pots weren't allowed until you reached your permanent camp.

One afternoon while most of the guys were playing cards down at one end of the room, I decided to make myself a cup of coffee. I poured water into a cup and set it on the floor beside my bed. Leaning over, I removed my stinger from beneath my mattress and eased it into the cup. I then carefully inserted one wire into the socket, stretching as far as I could. I got the wire halfway into the socket when it went "POW!" A cloud of smoke and a bunch of sparks flew out of the socket, and I let out a loud "Praise the Lord!" as I fell out of bed, landing on my already sore right leg!

A voice yelled out, "Hey, did you see that? Hicks must really be a Christian after all! Man, if I had gotten shocked like that, I would've been cussin' up a storm! But that cat's praisin' God! Man, he's one of them fanatics!"

After that afternoon's incident, my doubters slowly took a back seat to the inmates who believed in my stand. Oh sure, I continued to mess up now and then, but I was quickly discovering that every time I sinned now, I'd immediately get convicted. Then, after asking forgiveness, it was just as if I'd never even sinned. I got my peace back.

For example, one night some of the guys were gathered around Gene's bed where they were playing cards, telling jokes, and just passing time. One of them pulled out a joint of grass and lit it. When it got around to Gene, he offered it to me.

"No thanks," I said.

"Now come on, Christian, the Bible don't say nuthin' 'bout not smokin' weed," said Gene. "In fact, the good Lord woulden hav' put it on the earth if he didn't mean fer you to smoke it."

"Yeah," said another patient. "Why, the Bible even says 'let the earth bring forth grass and herb, and God said it was good!'"[13]

After they prodded me for awhile, I finally gave in, saying, "Well, I guess just a little won't hurt," taking a long hit off the joint.

It had been so long since I'd been high; my resistance was low, and I was out of it after only taking two tokes.

After that I slipped right into the middle of their conversation, exchanging jokes until it was time for lights out.

But then it hit me: Conviction City!

As I began to come down, I realized why it's not right to get high anymore. Because it's a trap by ol' slewfoot, so you'll let your guard down and freely sin!

I remembered some scripture Brother John Harber had once shared with me, which dealt with the consequences of a person getting drunk or high.

"Philip," John had said, "First Peter 5:8 reminds us to 'be sober, be vigilant; because your adversary the devil, as a roaring lion, walketh about, seeking whom he may devour.'

"In other words," he continued, "when a person gets drunk, whether it's with booze, drugs, or even illicit sex, then he or she falls into a situation that gets worse and worse and worse. One thing always leads to another, and before you know it, something or someone special to you has been destroyed. For this reason, it's so important to stay straight, and most important, stay prayed up. This way you'll be able to see temptation come your way, and you'll be able to resist it."

Slowly pulling the covers over my head, I began to pray. "Well Father, I have fallen once again, and I'm really sorry. I ask you to forgive me for getting high, and I thank you for doing so. Please help me be stronger in the future, so I won't be led astray so easily. And God, one more thing. Help me keep a clean testimony, so I can get the respect of these guys. I want them to come to know You, too, but they're gonna have to see that I'm different and that I have something they need before they'll want any of this Christianity business. Thank You, God. In Jesus' Name, Amen."

And as easy as saying a prayer, suddenly the guilt went away, and my peace returned. Soon I fell asleep.

✝ ✝ ✝

A few days later I got rid of still another habit.

Sitting up in bed reading my Bible, I reached over and got my only cigarette out of my bedside table, which I lit. Then, out of the corner of my eye I noticed Orlando staring at me from across the aisle. I thought to myself, *Boy, this sure must be some testimony*! I talk about a God that is so powerful, who does this miracle and that miracle, and yet I can't even get enough grace to quit these nasty cigarettes! Well, this is it! I'm quitting, and I'm not gonna wait until I finish this last smoke either!

Smashing it against the edge of the ash tray, I called out to Orlando, "Hermano, you got anymore of those lemon drops?"

"Sure, Felipe," he answered. "Here, you can have this whole bag." He tossed it across the room.

For a while it looked as if I had gotten hooked on lemon drops, but even that finally tapered off. And I never smoked another cigarette again.

One day I received a letter from Michael, my public defender. The following is a portion of that letter, which contained a long list of errors that had occurred during my trial:

> Dear Philip:
>
> I hope this finds you doing as well as can be expected. Hopefully you have now undergone surgery and will soon be walking again.
>
> Enclosed please find a list of the errors which occurred during your trial. These have been sent to the Appeals Court.
>
> Your state-appointed lawyer will use these errors in an attempt to vacate your sentence and get you a new trial.
>
> However, based on these errors, I don't really expect your sentence to be vacated. They are really very minor. Keep your faith, and maybe you'll be released after serving seven or eight years, provided your record stays clean.
>
> Sincerely, Michael

One of the inmates in my room was always working on legal stuff, and I heard he was pretty good at it. In fact, once another prisoner told me he was a jailhouse lawyer. One day I asked him about the list of errors and what he thought about my chances for a reversal.

"Hmmm," he paused, while checking out the letter from my P.D. "Looks to me like the only ground you got to stand on is points three and twelve, but that's only if there's any action from the Supreme Court."

"What's that supposed to mean?" I asked.

"Well," he explained, "about the only way you'll ever get back into court is if the higher court ever changes the law in regard to one of the issues, or errors, outlined here. In other words, they'll have to become reversible."

"How often do they change the law?" I asked.

"Based on the vast number of cases and errors argued, not very often," he continued. "It does happen, but don't start putting all your eggs in one basket. Wanna know what I think?" he asked.

"Yeah, sure," I answered.

"The State of Florida doesn't like anyone comin' from outta state and committing crimes. They have given you a heavy grudge sentence to teach you a lesson. But in a couple of years, you're gonna win a reversal based on one of these trial errors, and you're gonna return to court. Then they'll change your sentence to a flat ten years and release you with time served!"

As I was about to go to sleep that night, the list of errors came back into my mind.

For some reason, I felt real good about that list, and I do believe I was smiling as I drifted off to sleep.

✝

When a person receives Jesus as Savior, a battle begins in the spiritual realm for that person's soul. Satan doesn't want to give up another of his children. For this reason it is crucial for a young child of God to get serious about studying God's Word. For it reminds us that we're still going to sin but now we can ask forgiveness and still walk uprightly before God.

Even the Apostle Paul, whom God anointed to write much of the New Testament, encouraged us in Romans 7:15-17, "For that which I am doing, I do not understand; for I am not practicing what I would like to do, but I am doing the very thing I hate. But if I do the very thing I do not wish to do, I agree with the Law, confessing that it is good. So now, no longer am I the one doing it, but sin which indwells me."

While this doesn't justify a lifestyle of continuing sin, I'm encouraged that while my spirit man is ever changing, I will always have a sin nature—that is, until Jesus calls me home.✝

Philip's precious mother, Eleanor Hicks, and her three sons, Russ (Age 9), Jerry (Age 6), and Philip (Age 8)

Philip (Age 7)

Philip's high school graduation, May 1967

Victor Feliciano and Philip in the library of All-Souls Chapel at UCI

During the almost two years of Philip's stay at UCI, revival hit the prison and the brothers in blue were having CHURCH! God surely blessed them with some wonderful chaplains, including Eldon Cornett, Ronald S. Walker, Victor Morgan, and Larry Shook, not to mention the many programs and lay ministers who came in from the streets!

Philip was blessed and honored to have Victor Feliciano as one of his roommates. Because of his intelligence, amazing physical strength, dexterity in martial arts, and artistic abilities (an excellent painter!), Victor can best be described as a "Renaissance Man." But, most importantly, he now has a heart to please God! Much of Philip's growth during this time can be attributed to Victor for his constant encouragement and complete faith in our always-faithful heavenly Father!

Sister Dewella Williams and her ventriloquism dummy, Oscar! (The dummy is on the left and Philip is sitting on the floor.) Despite their divorce following a short marriage, Philip thanks God for His precious grace that has now reconciled them as friends. Now incorporated as d-vine ministries, Dewella faithfully ministers to children, families, and adults the world over!

Chelsie Hicks Williams (18) and her brother, Kyle (20), are now training for ministry through the Masters Commission at a church in Roseville, CA. They are surely two of the most wonderful children a man can have, and their deepest desire is to be found pleasing in God's sight!

Scooby the Clown (Linda Norris) and Rufus the Elf (Philip)

While these characters networked at a business function in 1990, Scooby introduced Rufus to one of the attendees, whose name was Patti Redeker. Following much healing and pre-marital counseling, Patti married the elf and became Patti Hicks in 1992!

Silly Philly (Philip) and Patticakes (Patti Hicks)

While Silly Philly has since traded his clown suit for a farmer's outfit (Cuz'n Philburt), Patticakes continues to bring God's love and laughter to children of all ages—at birthdays, carnivals, and churches!

Patti always wanted to become a clown, so she married one! Now she stays busy sculpting balloons and painting faces! Philburt was fired from painting faces 'cause he used a roller!

Patti and Philip adopted Cody two days after his birth in January, 1999! God desires to adopt each of us into His family!

For well over 13 years, Philip has combined "illusion, comedy, and amazing pig tricks" to captivate both children and adults while encouraging their spiritual growth! They love to uncover Bible truths in such stories as the Three Little Pigs, Charlotte's Web, and the Prodigal Pig!

Along the way, they've opened for such performers as Jeff Foxworthy and Juice Newton. They've appeared on the Carol Lawrence Show, Standup with Fred Travelena, and the Gabrielle Show, and entertained for the families of Mary Hart and Bill Paxton. They've also been featured on Los Angeles' KTLA-5 Morning Show and Sacramento's KOVR-13's Special Assignment! His hilarious hillbilly act won the Extreme Gong Show, performed regularly at the Gene Autry Museum, and delighted thousands while performing for corporate "pignics," schools, churches, and private events. Being from Memphis with the last name of Hicks, it's only natural that his standup shtick is titled "It's hard to be a hick in a hi-tech world!"

God has also inspired Philip to create and personify various other characters, such as Silly Philly the Clown, Grandpa Hicks, Elvis Hicks, Rufus the Elf, Lucky the Leprechaun, Professor Philburt, and Captain Cardio!

CHAPTER 18

DAY ONE AT THE ROCK

It was hard to believe that Christmas had already arrived. I had mixed emotions about this day because my parents were driving down from Memphis to visit me. I wanted to see them. And yet, I knew it would be especially rough on my mother. When I entered the visiting area, it wasn't hard to find them. My dad had already met some of the other visitors and prisoners. He was always the life of the party, and little children were especially drawn to him. One of them was already sitting on his knee, and he was singing to her.

"Hello, Mother," I whispered, as I put my hands on her shoulders.

Startled, she turned around. She gave me a kiss and a warm hug and said, "I love you, Phil."

By then, the little girl was off my dad's knee, and he put his arms around both Mother and me.

Despite the circumstances, I really enjoyed this. It seems like my dad and I were always distant, as if there was a wall between us despite ours being such a close and loving family. I think a lot of it was because he and I were alike in so many ways.

I realize now I had probably caused a lot of this, since I had rebelled against my folks so much. I had screwed up a lot, unlike my two brothers. The dark sheep of the family, I was always getting into petty stuff, and no doubt I had let my folks down a lot.

So it was pretty special whenever my pop would hug me.

"You've got another visitor who came with us," said my dad. "Turn around." I burst into tears of joy after turning around to see my younger brother, Jerry, walk toward us!

"What are *you* doing here?" I asked, as I grabbed Jerry and gave him a warm bear hug!

"You know I'd never turn down a trip to beautiful Florida!" Jerry replied.

A short time later, Jerry and I were talking at the snack bar while waiting on cold drinks.

"I can tell you're different," said Jerry.

"Yes, Jerry," I replied, "Jesus has set my heart free."

Considering the circumstances, we enjoyed a fairly good visit. I sure hated to see them go, but they had made plans to visit some of their Florida friends during the week, then they would return to see me the next weekend on their way back to Tennessee.

Little did any of us know that they'd be visiting me at a much different location the following weekend.

✝ ✝ ✝

Four days later, I was released from the hospital and transferred to "the Rock."

"Hicks, get up," said a loud voice from the doorway of my room. "You're being moved today."

Outside the window, it was still dark, and upon glancing at my watch, I realized it was only five o'clock in the morning. And yet, there on my bedside table was a breakfast tray. It contained a lukewarm container of milk, one hard-boiled egg, a bowl of prunes, and a cold piece of toast.

Nothing like breakfast in bed, I thought to myself.

✞ ✞ ✞

In less than an hour, I was sitting on a cold, hard bench in a large waiting room. Three other inmates, one guard, and I were waiting for another prisoner who was being brought over from hospital confinement. The guard and I were the only ones awake; the other guys were leaning against the concrete wall, snoring away.

After being frisked one more time, handcuffs were locked on each of us, and shackles were put on everybody but me. Since I was still walking with crutches, I guess they figured I wasn't much of an escape risk.

I'd heard it took less than an hour to reach the Rock, but it felt like a half-day trip to me. As we drove along, several thoughts popped into my head. My biggest concern was what my parents would think or do when they returned to Lake Butler and I wasn't there. The hospital chaplain had already advised me that once you reach your institution, there is a waiting period before you can have visitors. The normal process required visitors to write ahead and request visitor passes, and the institution would reply in a letter.

And now my folks would be driving up to visit me with no pre-approved passes. Already I could see my mother getting frantic.

I also thought about what Gene had once warned. His words echoed in my mind: "When you get to the Rock, you're gonna have to trade that Bible for a shank!"

Already I'd heard a lot of stories about the Rock. Actually, its real name was Union Correctional Institution. Located near Raiford, Florida, across the river from Death Row at Florida State Prison, the Rock was like a small city. Situated on seventy-eight acres, UCI housed close to two thousand men and had several different living areas. These included the West Unit, O Unit, Southwest Unit, the Flat Top, Medical Unit and

Psychiatric Annex, as well as the Main Housing Unit, also known as "the Rock." Surrounding the prison were three tall fences, each topped with barbed razor wire. The gun towers could be seen at short intervals, where armed guards stood on duty around-the-clock. The original facility, called the State Prison Farm, was established in 1913. Set on 18,000 acres, it housed 6,000 inmates, both male and female.

Any time you read something in the newspaper about Raiford, it usually dealt with bad news, such as someone being shot while trying to escape or about some problem inside the fences.

The public never heard about most of the violence that went on inside, however, including assaults and even murder. You never read about the men who walked in fear for their lives, who got paranoid every time it was time for lights out. You never read about the guys who got raped, nor about the drugs and buck (homemade liquor) that flowed freely. And you never read about the hate-filled gangs who seemed to live just to fight.

Yes, all I had heard about the Rock was negative—until I got inside the fences. I couldn't have known it at the time but, once again, the Lord had gone before me to make a few arrangements of His own to make certain His child's every need was met.

Our van rolled to a stop and as the door opened, I heard a gruff voice say, "New meat, boys." Another officer ordered us to get out. He was dressed in blue from head to toe, and he had an ugly-looking scar running the length of his face.

One of the guys behind me whispered, "Uh oh, there's Dragline."

"Who's Dragline?" another man asked.

"He's a 300-pound sergeant who drags his leg when he walks," replied the prisoner. "He'll beat your butt just for lookin' at him the wrong way. But I've heard he only does it to those who're in lockup, so there are no witnesses."

After being relieved of our handcuffs and shackles, we were told to grab our gear and line up against the wall.

One by one, each man was taken inside and strip-searched. Each man, that is, except me.

"Come with me," a gruff voice said. "You're going to the hospital."

It was none other than the guard they had called "Dragline," and he personally escorted me to the prison hospital.

On the way, I quickly discovered he wasn't as mean as the guys had said. In fact, because we both had something in common—injured legs—we seemed to have some sort of a bond between us. He seemed really interested in my injury.

Later on, I found out that he had indeed whipped some inmates in lockup, but usually it was because they had spit on him or called his mother names. In other words, most of the time they had provoked him.

After being examined by the prison doctor, he released me, saying there was no reason for me to be hospitalized. I agreed, because quite frankly, after 15 months, I'd had my fill of hospital life.

At the receptionist's desk, a lady told me an administrative aide was waiting outside to escort me to my cell. So, I crutched my way to the door and met a prisoner by the name of Tom, who stood beside a wheelbarrow full of my personal belongings, including my Bible and study books.

Tom stood almost six feet tall, with light brown hair that looked like it'd been recently styled. His bright blue eyes were highlighted by a continuous smile, and his white prison clothes looked as if they'd been recently starched and pressed. By the way he talked, I thought he'd surely graduated from a Dale Carnegie School.

As we headed over to my new home, he turned and said, "Well, Brother, I'm glad to have you here. God told me you were coming. We sure need some more sincere Christians."

Approaching my living quarters in an area known as the Southwest Unit, we walked under an overhang and stopped at a window, behind which sat a guard.

Two more guys, dressed in the same white clothes as those worn by Tom, walked up and introduced themselves. They seemed to be friends of Tom's, but they weren't as talkative as he. One of them asked for my measurements and said he'd order me a set of blues—prison clothes.

After Tom helped me up a short flight of steps into a building, I looked around and was shocked by the layout. Unlike the prisons I'd seen in the movies, I now stood on the second tier of a three-floor building, complete with air conditioning, color television, and a cold water dispenser!

But the thing that shocked me the most came next, when a guard assigned me a room—not a cell—and gave me a key.

After locating my room, I was surprised to discover there were no bars on the door. It was a solid door, sort of like you might find at the YMCA, except there was a narrow slit in it. I learned this was for the guards to look through when doing room checks, as well as for dispensing mail.

Opening the door, I discovered a fairly comfortable room. Tom unloaded my gear, and after I thanked him, he left. He returned a short time later and handed me two large containers—one with coffee and the other with sugar. "Thought you might enjoy this," he said, before leaving again. I lay down on my bunk and began reflecting on everything that had just taken place, when I heard my name paged over the loud speaker.

Grabbing my crutches, I headed up to the control room. One of the guards said, "Hicks, someone left this for you."

It was a foam-rubber pillow! Shaking my head in disbelief, I softly said, "Praise the Lord! This is just too much." I had a feeling it was Tom who left the pillow, but when questioned, all he said was, "Our Father knows our needs before we even ask."[14]

Of course, I didn't *need* a foam-rubber pillow, but that was the type I'd used most of my life. I had never cared for the feather-type.

And I was quickly discovering that oftentimes God does things—no matter how small—just to encourage His children and to remind them that He alone is faithful to meet and supply our every need.[15]

Right before lunch, I met my first roommate, Robert, who went out of his way to help me adjust to my new surroundings. This sure made my first day in the joint a lot easier.

Before I knew it, lunch and supper were behind us, and the television area was already packed. And then I heard an announcement that was music to my ears: "Line up for chapel!"

Since it was dark outside, I was surprised a guard didn't escort our small group to the chapel. Turning to a fellow walking beside me, I extended my hand and said "Howdy, my name is Philip."

"Hey Brother, Nightingale's the name, Mike Nightingale," he replied, as he warmly shook my hand.

"How come there's no guard escorting us?" I asked.

Mike shook his head and replied, "They must've checked the list, saw it was all regulars signed up for church and didn't see a need."

"I'm amazed that God gives such favor," I commented.

Groups of men joined us from different housing areas. By the time we reached the church, there were quite a few of us.

Even then, I thought it strange that my new brother, Tom, and his two friends hadn't joined us for chapel.

It's probably hard to believe, but on this particular night, I don't think I would have been any happier at a church "on the street" than I was right there in the prison chapel. Even before we went inside, I knew this was going to be an experience I'd long remember! Over a hundred yards from the chapel we could already hear the singing, and in the months and years to come, the song that was being sung, "Because He Lives," was to become my favorite Gospel hymn.

Nor did I ever expect what happened the moment I "crutched" into the chapel. As I walked inside, I looked straight ahead and couldn't believe my eyes. There was my old hospital friend, Orlando Gonzalez, and his eyes met mine at the same time!

"Felipe!" he screamed. "Mi Hermano, Dios de Bendiga!"

"Orlando!" I returned his greeting. It had been almost two months since I'd seen Orlando over at Lake Butler. It felt so great to see a familiar face, and he was equally excited to see mine.

Suddenly, it looked like my Cuban brother literally hurdled the two guys standing between us, as he gave me a big bear hug, exclaiming, "Felipe! I'm now a Christian!"

It must have been at least two hours before the service ended. And to say the least, we had church! It was one of the most beautiful services that I had ever attended. Come to think of it, it was my very first organized church service that I had attended as a Christian, and I had been a believer for well over a year.

While walking back to our housing areas, a small group of us were singing. In the background, we could hear another group singing the very same song.

As we approached my area, I asked one of the men if he knew Tom.

"Yeah, Brother, but Tom and his two friends don't attend chapel," he responded. "They kinda have church on their own. Do what you think is best, but I'd stay clear of that group, if I wuz you."

Later, I was to wish I'd heeded this brother's advice. But, as I was to discover, there'd be plenty of times that I'd ignore good advice until it was too late. But that's part of growing up, even as a Christian.

That night, as I lay on my new foam-rubber pillow, all I could say was, "Thank you, Father," over and over again. Seemed like I was getting blessed every time I turned around the entire day.

The surprises were only just beginning—and I had been in the joint less than a day!

Early the next morning I awoke to hear my name being paged once again. "Hicks, you have visitors! Hicks, you have visitors!"

This can't be me, I thought to myself. Surely they're talking about another Hicks. I had been told visitors had to write ahead for permission. And because this was a maximum security prison, security was a lot tighter than back at the prison hospital. And yet, an hour later I found myself sitting at a picnic table, enjoying a fantastic visit with my parents.

"How did you get in?" I asked my dad.

"Now, son, it seems like you used to include scriptures in your letters that went something like this: 'With God, all things are possible.'" We both laughed.

"Your father spoke to your classification officer at Lake Butler, and he cleared our visit through the administration here," said my mother.

I glanced back over at Pop, and already a little boy was sitting on his knee, listening to Pop sing a favorite song, "Well, Ole Joe Finney had 'em a pig, uh-huh-h-h-h, uh-huh-h-h."

Sometimes I wondered why God blessed me sooo much when others around me didn't seem to enjoy such favor and blessing. Looking at it from another perspective, I had

learned to be content in whatever situation I encountered and had been practicing the power of praise, regardless of my circumstances. So when I looked at something as a miraculous blessing and intervention of God, others failed to see the hand of God at work. Some believe they must prosper to be happy, but, personally, I was learning one of the greatest forms of prosperity was "to be content in whatever the situation."[16]✞

CHAPTER 19

TRIED BY FIRE

Before I knew it, the weekend was behind me and Monday morning had arrived.

It was barely 5:00 A.M. when our building got the call to line up for breakfast. This time we did get an escort to the chow hall, as the sun was not yet up. Rumor had it there'd been incidents in the past where inmates had slipped out of the line en route to breakfast, then hid in the shadows before making a dash for the fence. Few had made it. The ones that weren't buried ended up in the infirmary to be treated for buckshot wounds. They were then either hospitalized overnight or kept in confinement before being shipped across the river to Florida State Prison (FSP).

Although I had never been inside that institution, it was hard for me to believe any place was more fortified than the Rock! FSP was the home of the electric chair. They called it "Ole Sparky." Florida's Death Row housed some of society's most hardened criminals, and although it usually took years before their lives ended due to the lengthy appeals process, sooner or later they were destined to sit in the electric chair. That is, unless God intervened on their behalf. I had met at least two brothers in blue whose sentences had been commuted from Death Row to Life, and one had been miraculously released from prison!

On this day, I had to report to my classification officer. After he interviewed me, I waited in the hallway while he and a group of men considered my case.

"How much time you pullin'?" asked a prisoner sitting nearby.

Replying in some of the prison lingo I had now picked up, I said, "I got life plus a dime and a nickel, runnin' wild."

"It don't mean jack what the man giv' ya," said the prisoner, "cuz the parole board puts ya on trial all over again. They think they're God, and what they sez goes."

I soon discovered this man knew what he was talking about. And yet I also picked up that his faith was based on how much "good time" he could earn to shorten his sentence—definitely not on the God who promises to set the captives free.

Nevertheless, I was a little taken aback when my classification officer explained my tentative parole date.

"Because a gun was involved, you must pull at least a mandatory three-year sentence, plus the court required still another mandatory three years on both counts. And there are other factors which automatically aggravate your situation."

"What's that?" I asked.

"For example, someone was injured. Also, you'll have to pay restitution for the missing $5,000. Hmmm ... a number of people did write letters on your behalf, and it is your first offense; however, you have had several traffic citations in the past, which is not good."

"What does all this mean for me?" I asked.

"Let's see ... I'm going to set your parole date for October, 1986. I'll ask the board to give you credit for the time you spent in the hospital. If they approve, then you'll only do eight years and some change."

I gulped, swallowing thickly. I thought to myself, *Only eight years and some change from the prime of my life?*

"Of course, you'll be able to chop off a lot of this with days earned for working, good time, and for your participation in various programs ..."

I didn't even hear the last part, for all that echoed in my mind was October, 1986. Here it was, only December, 1979, and I was shot in September of 1978. That meant I would be off the street for more than eight years if I took this to their suggested parole date!

Stepping slowly between my crutches, I walked down the sidewalk away from the building and then stopped. A beautiful blue bird had flown right by me and landed on the sidewalk just a few inches away.

I stood still, admiring its beauty, when a Bible verse came to my mind. It had something to do with God caring for even birds, taking care of their every need. And if He cared about them, He cared about His children even more.[17] Then a verse came to my mind that said something about not worrying about anything and that I needed to take this to God in prayer 'cause He could handle my worries so much better than I![18]

Before I realized it, I was singing the chorus to my new favorite song: "Because He lives, I can face tomorrow ... because He lives, all fear is gone ..."

And then I found myself walking down the hallway of the chapel.

Knocking on the door, which was already open, I said, "Hello."

Rising quickly from his seat behind a large, cluttered desk, a short man with dark hair and glasses said, "Yes, may I help you?"

"I'm Philip Hicks," I said, "and I'd like to apply for a job as a clerk-typist in the chapel. I just arrived on Friday."

"My name is Chaplain Cornett," he responded, as we shook hands. "Actually, Mr. Hicks, we have a long list of persons who've expressed an interest in being assigned here, and we really have a full staff at present. You're welcome to sign up for chapel duty, but realistically speaking, there's quite a number ahead of you."

"Well, I'd like to add my name to the list anyway, just in case," I responded. I signed my name and housing location on the bottom of the long list of names the chaplain had laid before me.

After telling the chaplain it was a pleasure meeting him, I turned around and began to slowly "crutch" out of the office.

"Wait just a second," said a voice from behind me. "One of our clerks is away in outside court for a week, and there is a lot to be typed. Are you certain you'll be able to type, considering those crutches?" asked the chaplain.

"Why, there'll be no problem at all, Sir. After all, I type with my hands, not my feet!" I quipped.

He laughed before inviting me to follow him down the hall to an unoccupied room with a nice, big desk and a brand new typewriter. The floor shined like it had been freshly waxed. The room was filled with plants, and in the window was a large air conditioner.

"Here's where you can work until Nathaniel returns. If you have any questions, just ask," said Chaplain Cornett. He showed me what he needed typed and then he left.

Less than a week later the chaplain called me into his office. "Philip, as you know, our clerk has now returned," said Chaplain Cornett. "However, I've noticed you do very good work."

"Thank you, Sir," I replied.

"After careful consideration, we would like to assign you to the chapel full time," he said.

"Really? Oh, Praise the Lord!" I shouted.

"Who is your classification officer?" he asked.

I couldn't contain myself. I dashed over to the chaplain, crutches and all, grabbed his hand, and said, "Thank you, thank you, thank you! You won't be disappointed! Uh, oh, yes, my C.O.'s name is Robert Williams," I excitedly stammered before dashing out the door.

And that wasn't all. They even reassigned that private, air-conditioned office to me! Before long, it was filled with songs of praise and thanksgiving and became a popular stopping-off place for prisoners who were serious about their walk with God, as well as many hurting unbelievers.

✝ ✝ ✝

I soon learned why so many prisoners signed up to work at the chapel. Its air-conditioned environment was an oasis from the hot Florida sun, and clerks there were given extra gain time—time off one's sentence. Plus, there were usually plenty of refreshments, including freshly baked cookies sent in from the streets.

But most importantly, it proved the perfect environment for a Christian who really wanted to grow in his faith. Soon we had three chaplains who were so filled with God's Spirit that you'd think they'd already been raptured! And they were not only talkin' the Bible, but walkin' it, too. Could they teach!

From time to time, I'd stop by to visit Tom and his two friends. They'd always offer me a cup of coffee, and we'd engage in lengthy conversations. While I never noticed it at the time, I always did most of the talking, as Tom asked me question after question about my past life and the events following my conversion. I also didn't notice at the time, but Tom's two friends rarely spoke.

One of the chaplains, Ronald Walker, and I were talking one day about water baptism. Because of my injuries, I had not yet had an opportunity to be immersed in water, following the example of Jesus in water baptism. I was so excited when we set a March date for my baptism. We would've handled this earlier, but Chaplain Walker had to attend an Army Reserve camp.

But that was all right with me. The delay enabled me to write to my old friend, Brother Butch Ridgway, and ask if he and his wife, Kathy, could come up from Fort Lauderdale for a visit on this special occasion.

✞ ✞ ✞

Late one afternoon after work at the chapel I stopped by to visit Tom and his friends, George and Charlie. It was a visit I would soon regret.

After pouring myself a cup of coffee, I walked over and stood next to Tom, who had a Bible in his hands. George and Charlie were sitting at their desks. Tom began reading scriptures that he said pertained to me, yet they definitely weren't encouraging. Instead, I started feeling guilty.

After he read one in particular with which I was familiar, I interrupted, saying, "Hey, wait a minute, you're taking that verse out of context."

"Don't interrupt me, I'm getting off on this," he snapped at me, then continued his verbal attack. Then he said, "Mark 16:16 says 'He that believeth and is baptized shall be saved.' See, there it is, right there! Why, you haven't even been baptized yet, so you're not even saved!" Tom added.

That hit me like a lead balloon; I dropped my head in disbelief.

"And," Tom continued, "you've still got one foot in the world. You're still talking about your old girlfriend."

He came down on me about my old girlfriend so fast that I didn't even catch it when he said he was "getting off on this." I now know what God means when He promises to "give us a way to escape, so we can bear it."[19] But on that occasion, my mind was blinded by deception, and I was getting pulled under.

I started believing everything Tom said, and did he put a guilt trip on me. I even began to silently cry, thinking I wasn't even saved! I wanted to please God so very much.

"Listen," continued Tom, "the Lord has provided us a place right here on the compound to baptize those who wish to be obedient. Do you have any cutoffs?"

"Why, sure. I ..."

"Good!" he interrupted. "Bring a towel and meet us on the road beside the chow hall right after supper."

"OK," I responded quickly. I was beginning to see that there was hope again. "I'll be there."

An hour or so later, the four of us were turning onto the narrow sidewalk that ran in front of the building that combined both the vocational training and high school classes. Prisoners could also attend college classes in this same building during the evening. At that moment, the area looked empty.

We stopped beside a beautiful garden that bordered the front of the building. One thing that impressed the prison's visitors was the carefully manicured landscaping, maintained daily by the inmate-operated horticulture department.

"All right, step down into the water," directed Tom.

I looked down into the small pond of water that contained a few large goldfish, then glanced back at Tom. "You mean it?" I asked.

"You bet I do," replied Tom, "now hurry up before someone comes by and sees us."

I quickly stepped into the water, and Tom followed me, saying, "Now, kneel down."

I concentrated on Tom's words as he pushed me head-first into the cold, murky water.

"I baptize you in the name of the Father, and the Son, and the Holy Ghost," he said. He pulled me out of the water, and I looked around to see if anyone was watching. I saw two guys standing behind a tree, smoking a joint. Next to the building I saw another prisoner, standing with his "girl." In the joint, homosexuals were called "sissies" or "girls."

I saw all this going on, and here I was sneaking around, fearful that I was going to be caught while getting baptized! I instantly knew we were breaking the rules. The realization made me feel dirty and ashamed when I should have been feeling fantastic.

I didn't say a word as we walked back to the housing area.

When I was safely back in my room, I was on my knees beside my bed, repenting. I felt that I had sinned something awful. The fact that we were sneaking around gave the appearance of doing something wrong. On top of that, I always thought one needed a real preacher to do the baptizing, not a fellow inmate!

When I arrived at the chapel for work the next morning, I headed straight for the library to talk to Jessie, the chapel librarian. Jessie was known to be one of the most sincere, mature Christians behind the fence.

When I walked in the door, Jessie was sitting at his desk talking to John G., another very strong Christian who had been on the chapel staff for quite some time.

"Jess," I urgently said, as I approached his desk, "have you ever heard of a guy named Tom Baxter?"

I had barely spoken the words when both of them roared with laughter!

"Yeah," Jessie responded, "and you'd better watch out or he'll have you in the fish pond 'fore you know it!"

After the two of them laughed for a little while longer, I told them everything that had taken place since the day I arrived, when Tom was the first to greet me at Union Correctional Institution.

Then, it was their turn to explain why they were laughing.

It turned out that Tom had once worked at the chapel himself, and he had been respected as one of the strongest Christians on the compound. Somewhere along the line Tom got all puffed up with spiritual pride, and he thought he was better than everyone else. In fact, he thought he knew more than the chaplains.

Before long, Tom was slipping people up into the baptistery and baptizing them. When he was caught, he was fired as a chapel aide. But that didn't stop him! He then began baptizing people in a small fish pond out in front of the steam plant. Once he even baptized a guard. The guard was fired and the pond filled with dirt.

Tom had long since quit attending chapel services and had formed his own little cult. The group never grew very much, but in similar fashion to Guyana's Jim Jones, he had brainwashed quite a few along the way.

To be frank, the last thing Jessie and John G. told me made me feel a whole lot better.

"He took us to the pond, too!" added John G., "so don't feel too embarrassed."

Before I left, all three of us were laughing.

I soon learned that church behind the fences was no different than church on the street. Then again, ol' slewfoot's not too worried about the people outside church doors.

"He knows that if he can get the churches divided amongst themselves, then there'll be much less unity," said Jess during lunch one day.

"That makes sense," I agreed.

"In other words," he continued, "God's goal is to unite His church, while Satan works overtime in an attempt to bring division."

"He seems to be doing a fairly good job of that," I said.

"For in doing so, they're more likely to compare themselves with each other and start thinking things like 'our way or no way, us four and no more, etc.'" said John.

"How sad," I commented.

"It is sad," continued Jess, "and it's been goin' on like this since the beginning of the church. But one day, when the Lord returns to get His saints, there ain't gonna be anything like it is now. People are going to be surprised when they get to Heaven and find ex-Baptists, ex-Methodists, and even ex-Catholics!"

That evening I received an awesome letter from Brother Butch Ridgway down in Fort Lauderdale. It read:

Philly:

Joyful greetings in the name of our Lord! Hope ALL is going well with you as it surely is with us!

A few weeks after your sentencing, I talked with the Broward County Jail officials and asked to be allowed to conduct a weekly church service in the jail. Not only did they approve my request, but they also provided us with an entire cell! Then a local business donated a PA system, and I learned that because of the sound system, the music and preaching could be heard all over the jail!

We've called it "The Potter's House," and a funeral parlor has donated chairs. So where the chairs were formerly used by people who came to pay their last respects to the dead, they are now being used by people who are discovering new life!

Great things are happening in the Potter's House! Men are being saved, healed, and set free from all types of habits!

There's one fellow named Eddie, who was illiterate; he could barely read or write. Recently he was baptized in the Holy Spirit. Before long he began reading and understanding the Bible. And now, he has memorized almost the entire Gospel of John! I've asked him to write to you, so expect his letter soon!

Keep the faith! Love, Brother Butch

P.S. Kathy and I are planning to visit you. We'll keep you posted.

By this point, nothing amazed me when it came to God being at work in our midst! I recalled how the jail sergeant insisted that "Butch will never again visit this jail!" God had another plan.

✞ ✞ ✞

If records had been kept at the joint, I probably set a new record for the largest number of different roommates, as I went through no less than nine during my first six months in prison.

To say the least, none of us had much in common, as there were very few who were as sold out for the Lord as myself. But one thing I do know, before my roommates departed through that revolving door, at least seeds of the Gospel were being planted in their minds, if not in their hearts.

By this time, I knew better than to preach at anyone. I just let my walk match my talk, and without fail, sooner or later they would ask a question pertaining to the Bible. That gave me an open invitation to tell them how I had been introduced to God.

Before long, I had grown to expect certain questions, which guys would ask in an effort to trip me up and even get me to wondering why God does certain things the way He does.

But as time passed and I grew more mature as a Christian, I realized that God would indeed put His words in my mouth in order to glorify Him. An example of this happened one morning.

"Hey man," said Ernie, one of my first cell-mates, "if God is as all powerful as you say he is, then how come he don't just drop out of the sky and git rid of all the evil?"

"Well Ernie," I answered, "God really wants to do just that, and soon He will. But if He did it right now, millions of people would be destroyed along with Satan and his crowd. Yet, thousands are being saved in the meantime, and God wants you to be one of them."

Another popular issue that often surfaced was marijuana. In fact, I sure wish I had known more scripture when I was in the hospital, back when I screwed up and got high, all because a guy used the Bible to make me think it was all right. A Christian brother, or at least a professing Christian, once asked, "What's wrong with smoking marijuana, man? The Bible says in Genesis 1:29 that 'God gave man every herb bearing seed,' and marijuana is an herb."

But I since learned that this was before the fall of Adam and Eve. Their sin was followed by a curse on the ground, bringing forth thorns and poison plants. If one continues to read, and doesn't take it out of context, Genesis 3:17 spells it out loud and clear! In other words, there's a snake in the grass—Satan!

The Bible classifies drugs, even consciousness-changers like marijuana—under sorcery. The Greek word for sorcery is *pharmakeia*. The word "pharmacy" comes from this word. The books of Isaiah and Revelation shed further light on this.

✞ ✞ ✞

One night I was lying on my bunk when I heard a loud noise, and it wasn't coming from outside my door. I stood up and walked to the sink, paused for a moment and looked up at the vent on the wall. I heard the scraping noise again, followed by voices.

The door suddenly swung open. My roommate and two other guys ran into the room.

"Get outta the way!" my roommate ordered. Stepping up on the toilet, he was already using a shank to remove the vent cover.

Turning to one of his friends, he whispered, "Start whistling if you see the hack!"

I looked back up at him and saw he had his entire arm stretched inside the open vent.

"OK, I got it," he whispered, and he slowly stepped to the floor.

In his hand was a bleach bottle. But that wasn't all! A string was tied to it, which he began pulling out of the vent. Another bleach bottle appeared. Then another, and another… and still another!

When he got through, I counted nine bottles of bleach, but of course I knew those bottles weren't full of bleach.

They grabbed the bottles and ran out. Less than a minute later came an announcement over the loud speaker: "Everyone go to your rooms! This means everyone ... immediately!"

Loud cursing and complaining followed from a few men whose Monday night movie had been cut short. Nevertheless they folded their chairs and returned to their rooms. Just before the automatic locks were snapped on each door by the guard in the control room, in walked my roommate.

"Whew!" he let out a gasp of breath. "That was a close one! That would've been a real bummer. That 'buck' has been fermenting for over a month!"

A short time later, two guards entered our room, and the standard shakedown procedure began. The last thing they checked was the vent, which was now empty.

Once again, I thought, there'll be some drunk inmates this weekend. But who was I to judge? Before coming to Christ, I, too, had attempted to fill my emptiness with everything under the sun—mostly illegal substances. But nothing ever seemed to satisfy.

And sooner or later a man is gonna get caught. What goes around comes around.[20] And yet, the Bible also reminds us the upright should never stand in the way of sinners.[21] So if my roommate and his friends ever got busted, I wasn't around to find out. Shortly thereafter, he was transferred to another unit.

I was often reminded that we're each to "work out our own salvation with fear and trembling." I kept this in mind as I observed others worshiping God in the manner they

felt most comfortable. So whether a person declares himself Christian or Muslim, Protestant or Pentecostal, he or she has the free will to believe as they wish—and it was not my position to judge another for his or her beliefs.

I had also learned the all-important lesson that as I pursued God with all of my heart, my Father would equip me with every gift necessary to fight the good fight of faith and walk in victory.✞

CHAPTER 20

REFINED BY FIRE

"Buck" is the name given to homemade liquor. It doesn't matter how secure a prison, the buck never stops being made. Just like marijuana and other drugs, if a person has the money, this homemade liquor is available. 'Bout the only thing you can't get into an all-male prison is women, but beggars can't be choosy. Oftentimes a man is forced into becoming a "girl."

Many a sincere Christian has been tested behind prison walls, just to find out if he or she is real or not. And one of the most common ways he's tested is through his manhood.

My case was no exception. My major test took place on the day of my glorious water baptism—a day I had long awaited. Chaplain Walker had scheduled it for March 3. Brother Butch and Sister Kathy had driven up from Fort Lauderdale to visit and to witness my special mountaintop experience.

And this time, when I came up out of that water, I did indeed feel like a new man. This time there were no fish in the tank with me, but even that wouldn't have mattered.

After the church service, I spent over three hours in the visiting park with my friends. Butch bought me a made-to-order cheeseburger from the snack bar, another highlight of the day. It was fantastic! A person takes store-bought food for granted until it's no longer available. We all take things like this for granted until we cannot access them.

My heart was aching when it was time to say good-bye, but I knew that we'd see each other again.

After they left, I returned to the dressing room to change into my prison blues. While in the park, you have to wear prison whites, which you return following your visit. Of course, you also get strip-searched, to make sure your visitors didn't smuggle any drugs or green money to you. The latter is also considered contraband; the only money an inmate is allowed to have comes in the form of coupons.

On the way back to my cell, I was having a good old time, singing and humming and thanking God for treating me to such a wonderful day.

Since that time, I've learned over and over to always be on the alert, for often after a Christian enjoys a mountaintop experience, old slewfoot will attempt to steal your joy. This particular day was no different.

In my cell, I stretched out on my bunk, propped my arms behind my head, and began reflecting on all the fantastic things that had happened throughout the day.

There was a knock on the door. Looking up I saw a face in the door slit that I didn't recognize; but that didn't make any difference. I got up and opened the door, saying, "Howdy, what can I do for you?"

"Listen man, I need to talk to you," said the stranger, who seemed friendly enough.

I sat on the edge of my bed and said, "Yeah, what's going on?"

Suddenly, this rather tall, stout-looking fellow changed the tone of his voice and angrily declared, "Listen, dude, I was in the chapel for the Catholic service yesterday, and a visitor slipped me twenty bucks green. Well, I got busted and a guy told me you snitched me out! I want my money, and I want it now!" he screamed as he pushed up against my leg with his own.

Surprising even myself, I calmly answered, "Man, I have never seen you before, and while I do work at the chapel, I have never attended the Catholic service. Plus, I'm not a snitch and I don't have any money."

He ripped off his shirt and continued, "Don't give me any of that crap! Now I'm gonna give you five minutes to get my money; and if you don't get it, I'm gonna whip your butt all over this cell!" He then grabbed his shirt and split, slamming the door behind him. I didn't know why he gave me five minutes or where he went, but that didn't matter. I knew only that it was time to do some serious praying![22]

"Now God," I began, "you know I'm not afraid of this guy, but I also don't want to ruin my Christian testimony by swapping hands. Now I just don't know what to do, so you're going to have to handle this if I'm going to be able to stand up for what I believe."

Lying very still, a scripture suddenly came to mind that says something like: "Greater is He that is in me than he that is in the world."[23]

I spoke to God: "Well, Father, I do believe that verse is true, and I'm gonna stand by that promise, but I really need You to keep me calm and help me with the right words to say, and what to do, and all that. And most importantly, God, whatever happens, don't let this guy think I'm a sissy 'cause I won't swap hands with him, OK? I want these people to respect me."

He knocked on the door a few minutes later. "Open this door, now!" he screamed.

Well, I thought to myself, this cat may think I'm scared, but one thing's for sure, I ain't stupid. If he thinks I'm gonna let him in again, he's lost his marbles!

"Why don't you just go away, man? I told you I don't know anything about your money," I responded quietly. He cursed loudly and took off. I returned to praying.

"Now God," I continued, "it's hard to believe that this thing has ended so easily, but I do know You're in the miracle-working business, and this may very well be another one of Your solutions. Whatever happens, thank You very..."

I was interrupted by the noise of my door being unlocked, and I looked up to see this same guy hurriedly walk into my room. Somehow, he now had a key!

"OK, punk," he jeered. "Where's my money? I want it now!"

In ran my roommate and another inmate, who sat down on my roommate's bed. Glancing at each other, they smiled but didn't say anything.

I was now sitting across my bed, with my back against the concrete wall, my legs hanging over the side.

As my attacker pushed against my legs with his own, he cursed loudly, demanding his money and threatening to break my nose and a few other things.

"Listen," I said, "I just want you to know that I'm not mad at you because you've accused me of something I didn't do. I want to be friends with you. I'm now a Christian and because of this, I love you and everyone else, and I don't want to fight with anyone."

"Oh, so you love me, huh?" he said. "Well," he continued, "if you love me, then maybe you wanna be my girl!"

At that, my roommate and his buddy began laughing uncontrollably.

I didn't say a word in reply to this last remark, yet deep inside I knew this was going to be the real test.

I began silently praying in the Spirit, and all at once I felt a real strange peace come over me, and I knew I wasn't alone.

As the man continued to scream at me, he stuck his pointed finger up against my face and I could feel his fingernail digging into my skin.

All I could think of was a picture I'd recently seen of the Lord before he was crucified, with the crown of thorns rammed down upon his head and blood streaming down his face.[24]

I knew this little fingernail that now pierced my own skin was nothing, nothing at all, compared to what my Savior had experienced.

"You can do anything you want to my body, but you can never touch my soul,"[25] I quietly said.

"Whaddaya mean I can't touch your soul? Why you ..." he said.

"That's right, man!" my roommate suddenly interrupted. "That's right, man. There's something in the Bible about that!"

My roommate had spent a lot of time in the Flat Top, and all they allow a person when in maximum security is a Bible. Of course, when tiring of reading it rumor has it they also use the thin paper to roll cigarettes!

As my would-be attacker stepped back, I stood up and faced him. I began trying to walk past him, but he kept moving from side to side, blocking my way. I could tell he was just trying to get me to make the first move, so he'd have reason to unload on me.

I whirled around, laid my Bible on the bed and said, "Man, you can do whatever you gotta do, but I'm leaving this room right now!"

My roommate said to his buddy excitedly, "Aw right! See, I told you!"

I then began to pray out loud, stopping to occasionally say, "Praise the Lord! Glory to God! Praise You, Jesus!"

Next, the strangest thing happened. The inmate who blocked my path stepped aside and screamed, "Shut that up! Shut up! Go ahead, you can leave but shut up that crap!"

I took a step toward the door, then hesitated, pivoted on one foot, faced my attacker and said, "Why, I'm not goin' anywhere. This is my room, and I'm staying right here! Glory to God forevermore!" I began singing in the Spirit and repeating, "Praise You, Jesus! Praise You, Lord Jesus." Covering his ears with his hands, he screamed, "I can't stand that!" and he ran out the door, followed by my roommate and his buddy.

To my surprise, when I looked outside my cell, people were lined up and down the hallway, even standing up and down the stairs that were outside my room. Quietly closing my door, I again lay down on my bunk and you can believe I began praying again. Only this time it was a prayer of thanksgiving.

A couple hours after chow that evening, I was again lying on my bunk when there was still another knock on the door. I could hardly believe my eyes when I looked up and found that same guy at my door again. I didn't even hesitate, rising quickly to open the door.

"Listen, man," he began, "we're making sandwiches upstairs and ... uh ... we're kinda short on bread. Could you spare a few slices?"

Smiling on the inside, I responded, "Well, I don't have but a few slices left but...sure, you can have them." From under my bed, I pulled out the old shoe box where I kept my bread and peanut butter.

After accepting the bread, he turned to leave, but then he stopped. Looking at the floor, he mumbled softly, "Listen ... uh ... I just want you to know that, well, I'm sorry about this afternoon. I talked to my cousin again, and he said you weren't the one who snitched me out after all."

"Hey, that's OK," I answered. "You were forgiven the moment you left the room. Hey, man, if I couldn't forgive you, then Christ would never forgive me for all the times I've screwed up."

As I began telling this guy about the things that had happened to me, he sat down on our only chair—the commode seat—and intently listened. After awhile I asked him the same question that Ken had asked me way back in that Fort Lauderdale hospital room: "Do you know for certain, that if you were to die tonight, that you would go to Heaven?"

As he began to respond, we heard yelling coming from the stairs, "Hey, hurry it up! We're starving up here! What's taking so long, homeboy?"

"Oh, I gotta go … listen, thanks again for the bread … er … I'll pay you back," he said. Then he left.

Strange how things happen sometimes. This guy came for a few slices of bread, but he left having heard about the Bread of Life. And no, he never repaid what he borrowed, but that doesn't matter. What goes around comes around. In other words, a man's going to reap what he sows, whether he believes it or not.

And speaking of reaping, a few days later a guard told me I had lost my roommate. Both he and his buddy, and the dude who'd threatened me, had been caught hiding escape paraphernalia, including two ropes and a set of wire cutters, plus half a pound of weed. All three were sent across the river to Florida State Prison.

Later on I also learned that business about the Catholic service was all a lie, and the whole thing a set-up. All they had in mind was to find out just what I was really made of, whether I was for real or just another phony Christian trying to hide behind the Bible or trying to use God.

But as Chaplain Shook once pointed out in a sermon, "God is not mocked. It's impossible to use God. If any of you are masquerading as a Christian, you can be sure your sins will find you out. Sooner or later you'll slip up, and somebody watching you is going to write your ticket."

And speaking of being watched, it doesn't matter if you're a professing Christian in the joint, at a Christian university, a member of a church, or whatever. The Bible reminds us that we're going to be continually watched and "read" by others. They want to know if what we got is real or not. If it is, more will be added to the Kingdom … but if it ain't, a person is gonna lose their respect real quick, and in some cases, possibly their life.

After the incident when the inmate threatened me about the money, I soon learned that AT&T has got nothing over the communication system in the joint. Seemingly overnight, people all over that 2,000-inmate prison had heard about what happened, and consequently, I gained respect from many who then knew that my walk matched my talk. In the joint, that's something to be proud of 'cause it don't matter how bad a guy professes to be—it takes a real man to walk with God in the middle of Satan's playground. And to be a real man, it's crucial to lay aside one's pride and reputation and allow Christ to live *His* life through you![26]

While my faith had grown tremendously through my hospitalization and court trial, nothing compared to experiencing the ordeal of being threatened with bodily harm ... and seeing firsthand the power of praise at work!

The scripture "out of the mouth of babes thou hast ordained power to still the avenger" rang so true that day as the God who "inhabits our praises" won a major victory over the spirit of darkness that lived within my oppressor! "Not by might, nor by power—but by My Spirit," says the Lord.✝

CHAPTER 21

HEALING

During my first year at Raiford, I was taken to the University of Florida Shands Teaching Hospital on three different occasions to be checked out by my doctors.

Prior to the third trip there, I was returned to the Lake Butler hospital to have the pins removed from my leg.

By my third visit to Shands, even my doctors were amazed at my progress and how well my fractured bone had become realigned and had grown together.

"I must admit," said Dr. Hankins, "considering the extent of your break, I never once thought your femur would look this good again."

As he held up the x-ray, I, too, was amazed by the healing process. In fact, because of the extra bone transferred from my hip bone, my leg now looked stronger than ever!

After returning to Raiford, I told Chaplain Shook.

"Unbelievers would look at this as another miracle, Philip," began the chaplain, "but as Christians we can accept it as still another one of our heavenly Father's promises. In 3 John 2 we are reminded God wants His children 'to prosper, both materially and physically, but only as their souls prosper.' For you see, if our souls don't mature in Christ, then it's likely we won't be able to handle material prosperity. And, even if we receive a physical healing, we're liable to forget about God and give the credit to the doctors."

✞ ✞ ✞

Between my trips to the hospitals and the loss of different roommates for various reasons, I must admit I longed for a sincere Christian roommate.

My prayer would soon be answered, but first I had to wait for my roommate-to-be to get saved. This happened in the strangest way.

Following a special chapel service one Saturday afternoon, I was standing near the front entrance when who walked up but Orlando, the proud Cuban whom I'd met while in the hospital, and who had later given his heart to the Lord after arriving at Raiford.

"Felipe," said an excited Orlando, "this is Victor. He wants to become a Christian!"

"Well, praise the Lord," I responded. "Why don't the three of us go down to the altar and talk?"

While talking to Victor, I discovered he was born in Puerto Rico but now lived in Miami ... that is, until he got busted. Despite attending a Catholic church most of his life, Vic had never truly become a born-again Christian.

"Orlando," I said, "why don't you lead Victor in the sinner's prayer?"

It didn't require asking a second time, as the three of us immediately knelt to pray.

As Orlando led us in prayer, I joined Victor in repeating, "Heavenly Father, I know that I have done a lot of bad things. I have sinned against You, and I need to be forgiven. Jesus, I thank You that You died on the cross for me. Thank You for paying for every one of my sins. I open the door of my heart and invite You to come in. I receive You and Your forgiveness into my life right now. Fill me with the Holy Spirit and empower me to live for You. Thank You for saving me! In Jesus' name, Amen."

"Gloria adios!" shouted Orlando, as a grinning Victor wiped away tears. "Victor," Orlando encouraged, "this will be a day you will always remember!" Then we gave each other a big hug.

"Hey Victor," I suggested, "why don't you write your daughter and tell her of your decision?"

"Great idea, Felipe," responded a very excited Victor, "but first, I want to go tell Chaplain Shook of my decision."

It's not necessary that another person join you when asking the Lord into your heart. It's just that, sometimes it's encouraging when others join a person in this prayer, so they're reminded of their new family.

Speaking of family, I was constantly being reminded of how small this world really is, especially when God's family covers it. For example, one Sunday afternoon following chapel, I struck up a conversation with two guests from Mississippi. Scottie and Sandra were in Florida to visit their uncle, Chaplain Shook.

"Did you say you were originally from Memphis?" asked Sandra.

"Why yes," I answered.

"What part of Memphis are you from, and what church did you attend?" asked Scottie.

"I grew up in North Memphis, in an area called Frayser, where I was a member of Schoolfield Methodist Church," I replied.

"By any chance, are your parents Buck and Eleanor Hicks?"

"Why yes, how did you know, Sandra?" I asked excitedly.

Now grinning from ear to ear, she said, "Well, because we used to live in Memphis, and not only did we attend Schoolfield, but I also worked with your mother at the hospital. Your parents are good friends of ours!"

Now speechless, all I could do was give them both big hugs before rushing off to tell Chaplain Shook! After this, my friendship with Brother Shook became stronger and stronger. In fact, he became like an uncle to me.

Early one Saturday morning I awoke early—if 7:00 A.M. can be considered early—so I could hit the canteen line before it got too long. Our building was called out for chow at around 5:30 A.M., but hardly anyone got up to eat breakfast on Saturdays. Considering what was usually served, you'd think the cooks skipped it, too. The Saturday menu normally consisted of one cold hard-boiled egg, one rather damp piece of toast, and some real weak coffee. Don't get me wrong—chow is usually right on time, but not on Saturday mornings. Besides, the guys with money in their accounts drew their canteen money on Friday nights; thus, the canteen line was always long come Saturdays.

On this particular morning, as usual, some of the Blacks and Hispanics were already exchanging heated words. Most of the violence in the joint was caused by the ongoing hatred between black and Hispanic people. When fights erupted everyone suffered, as the joint was always locked down, resulting in loss of privileges until tempers cooled.

Normally I just accepted this as part of prison life, but on this particular morning it was hitting close to home because an inmate was challenging my new Christian brother, Victor, to fight.

"Don't mess with me or you'll be sorry!" yelled Victor.

"I'm gonna show you who's tha sorry one. I got something for you, Hermano," threatened a tall, muscular inmate.

"Chill," interrupted someone, "here comes tha hack!

In the yard later on, I saw Victor and Orlando. As I approached them, I knew things were not cool, because they were doing some heavy talking in Spanish. In fact, for a moment I thought Victor was mad at Orlando.

"Es en negro no me ba a mandar!" screamed Victor.

"Te vas a meter en proglemas y te van a enserar!" replied Orlando.

"Ami no me importa," said Victor.

"Yo soy un hombre oya voy a sacar una fila."

Orlando continued. "Ya eres Christian no puedes aser eso, deja que Jehovah se encarge."

"Anybody for a game of handball?" I interrupted. "There's a court empty, but we'd better hurry ... "

About that time the horn sounded for the yard to be cleared.

While talking with Orlando later that day, I learned that Victor had a plan for dealing with the inmate who had hassled him in the canteen line. He was going to get a shank and be ready the next time the guy sold out to him.

Orlando had warned Vic that he'd get into trouble and get locked up. When Vic insisted he was a man and could take care of himself, Orlando reminded him that he was also now a child of God and that God would take care of him.

When Vic sarcastically asked Orlando if God was going to come down out of the sky, Orlando assured him that God's angels are sent to protect Christians.

I saw Victor a couple times over the next week and I could tell he was under a lot of pressure. I could relate to the battle that was going on inside him, and yet, something told me that this young man was going to make it in his walk with God, even here in the joint.

"Hey Vic," I said one afternoon while standing out in front of our housing areas, "my roommate moved out yesterday and ... er ... what would you think about moving in with me, that is, if the man approves it?"

"Say, that would be good," responded Vic, "only I hear it's real difficult to get a room change."

"Well," I said, "let's agree in prayer that it'll get approved, OK?"

"Sure, man, sure," said Victor before walking off.

I picked up that Victor doubted the transfer request would get approved, and he had good reason to doubt. Because of the heavy homosexuality that went on in the joint, the administration was real leery of men who wanted to change rooms. In fact, about the only way an inmate could change rooms was if he got busted or if he slipped an officer some green.

And yet, I'd seen God work so many, many times in the past ...

✝ ✝ ✝

Less than a week later, as I was checking in at the control room, the sergeant motioned me to come inside.

"Hicks," he said, "I don't know how you did it, but Feliciano's request for a room change got approved. Tell him to get it packed and be moved before chow."

"Thank you, Sir, thank you very much," I responded. By now I knew better than to bring anything up about God around this particular officer, but inside I was about to bust because I knew exactly who was responsible for this room change, and earth was not His only home!

As he unpacked the final box of his belongings later that evening, Victor said, "Felipe, I never would've believed it if it hadn't happened. Jehovah really does look out after His children."

"Yeah, He sure does Vic, and in fact," I said, "He's also powerful enough to protect His children. 'Cause if He didn't, then we'd have to rely upon shanks to protect ourselves."

"Yeah, maybe you got a point there, Felipe...you just might have a point," said my new roommate.

After lights were out later that night, Vic and I were talking. "You know, Vic, I couldn't ask for a better anniversary present than this," I said.

"Huh, what you mean, Felipe? Are you flippin out, man?"

"Well," I said, "in one week I will have been here exactly one year...and I finally got a Christian roommate!"

I didn't know then how strong a Christian Vic was to become, or how long he was to remain my roommate. Nevertheless, that night I fell asleep a very happy man.

One of my favorite scriptures is in 3 John 2, which says "Beloved, I wish above all things that you prosper, and be in health, even as your soul prospers." While I learned God chooses when and how to heal, I was humbled that my leg had healed so wonderfully. My heavenly Dad finally blessed me with a Christian roommate and, once again, exceeded my expectations as He brought a couple to visit—all the way from Memphis—who were friends of my parents.✞

CHAPTER 22

CHANGE IS GOOD

It didn't take long to discover that Vic and I were the perfect roommates.

We stayed busy and time flew by! Vic's job assignment was at the high school, where he taught Spanish and English. We both enjoyed working out with weights and running, so we stayed in tip-top condition. It had been months since I had laid my crutches aside, and my injured leg grew stronger by the day.

Of course, Vic was already in condition when he came off the streets. After serving in the Marine Corps for four years, he returned to Miami, where he worked as a lifeguard on Miami Beach, keeping in shape by lifting weights and practicing karate. A straight "A" student at Miami-Dade Junior College, he continued his education at American University. During this time, he got busted.

Vic and I began meeting another inmate named Tank three days a week at the weight pile to work out. One day a fourth man joined our group.

"Just a little more. C'mon, you got it! That's it! Praise the Lord!" I shouted as Vic pushed the barbell upward one final time.

"Whew," he grunted, the sweat pouring off him.

"Man, that was 250 pounds!" I exclaimed.

"I can do all things through Christ," said a beaming Vic.

"Yeah, but you hardly weigh even 140 pounds!" I added.

"Hey, do you guys mind if I join you?" questioned a voice from behind me.

Turning around, I immediately recognized the owner of the strange voice, and quite frankly, I didn't know how to respond, 'cause I didn't know what Vic would say. It was the same black guy who had been on Vic's case in front of the canteen several weeks earlier. What happened next kind of shocked me, and it sure made me proud of my roommate.

"Sure, man," Victor said, "you can do a set of benches now, 'cause we've already done two sets. Here, I'll spot you."

At first I wasn't sure if Vic was going to drop the weights on the guy's head. Quietly, I began to pray.

After our newest workout partner finished his set, and his head was still together, he turned to Vic and said, "Thanks, man."

While the new guy was spotting for Tank, Vic turned to me, smiled, and said, "Well, Felipe, Jehovah really does make your enemies to be at peace with you."[27]

Turning to acknowledge Vic's outstretched high five, I said, "Si, Hermano, Si."

✞ ✞ ✞

The fantastic chaplain who had water-baptized me well over a year before, Chaplain Walker, had since left UCI to become Head Chaplain across the river at Florida State Prison, where Death Row is located.

Talking to Chaplain Cornett one Monday morning, I asked, "How is Chaplain Walker doing over at Florida State Prison?"

"He's doing just fine, Brother Hicks," said the chaplain.

"Well, when are we going to get a new chaplain?" I asked.

"He's due to arrive sometime next week."

"What's his name?" I questioned.

"His name is Victor Morgan," continued Chaplain Cornett, "and this'll be his first assignment as a prison chaplain. He's fresh out of seminary."

One week later I had the pleasure of being the first inmate to meet and talk with our new preacher, and I immediately knew the guy was for real. It was common knowledge in the chain gang that there were some chaplains who were unsaved and were working just to have a job. Later on I learned that even on the streets there are men working in churches that are not called to pastor, nor do they enjoy a personal relationship with God.

"Hello Brother!" exclaimed a warm, friendly slim black man, as he excitedly shook my hand.

"Chaplain Morgan," I said, "we are awful glad to have you here."

"Glad to be here, Brother!" he responded.

As we got to know each other, I learned Brother Morgan was raised in nearby Jacksonville, where he, too, had tried to find happiness in drugs and women, but the Spirit of God wouldn't let him get away.

"I was a member of the Church of God in Jesus Christ," said Brother Morgan.

"Well, that title sure covers all the bases!" I said, as we both laughed.

Soon Brother Morgan's lovely wife began attending Sunday morning chapel with us and would often bless us by singing.

And speaking of singing, I doubt seriously if any prison in the entire state, or in the entire country for that matter, had as many ministry groups coming inside to bless and encourage us with much singing and preaching.

At least twice a year the Bill Glass and Jim Wilson Crusades visited for two and three days at a time. Plus, Abe Brown's Prison Group and several others visited annually. Campus Crusade for Christ also had a prison outreach, called P.S. Ministries.

P.S. Ministries was committed to discipling the lives of both men and women behind bars. Because of their in-depth approach and dedication to making certain new Christians became rooted and grounded in their faith, many never returned to prison after they left.[28]

One morning I shared my testimony with Jim Marsh, the man who headed P.S. Ministries, and afterwards he gave me some solid advice.

"Philip, God has a special calling on your life, and you're going to be used mightily in some type of ministry for Him. Now some men are able to stay single, but after hearing all about your background, you'll definitely be getting married one day."

"Alleluia," I shouted, "that works for me!"

"Do yourself a favor. After you get out, take time to get to know yourself again. Allow yourself some time to get used to living as a Christian out on the streets. Don't go looking for a wife.

"If you put God first, your all-knowing heavenly Father will provide you with the soul-mate of His choice. But it's important that you know for sure she's God's choice!

"Attend church and Bible study with her. Get to know everything about her—her likes and dislikes, weaknesses, etc. Let her get to know your shortcomings, etc.

"Make sure the relationship is anchored in the Lord, 'cause if it is, then it will last."

"Thanks, Brother," I responded, "you have much wisdom. But what about you, Jim?" I asked. "Why did you get married?"

"Quite frankly, I wasn't looking for a wife at all, when Susie came along," responded Jim. "Why, I didn't even kiss her, much less hold her hand, for close to a year. Just wasn't seeking a wife at all. But deep inside, we both knew. And it'll be the same way for you. You'll know.

"Now, let's lift your need up to the Father. Heavenly Father, we now ask You to begin preparing Philip a wife, a wonderful helpmate. While Philip is incarcerated, we ask You to begin molding her, so that when it's Your perfect time for them to become one, they will be perfectly matched. In Jesus' name we thank You, Amen."

✞ ✞ ✞

With all the crusades, my chapel work was heavier. The busier I stayed, the faster time flew by. Right in the middle of it all, revival broke out at Union Correctional Institution. Oftentimes, as many as a dozen Christians lined up on Sunday mornings to be water baptized. No, not in the fish pond; they did it right.

One day Brother Morgan called me into his office.

"Sit down, Brother, we need to talk," he said. "Brother Philip," he began, "since being here I've grown to recognize you as one of the strongest Christians on this compound. You've got a lot of young Christians, as well as older ones, looking up to you and following your example."

As Brother Morgan continued to heap praise on me, I noticed he began slowing down, choosing his words more carefully, and I knew something was up. He hadn't called me in just to inflate my ego. I knew better than that.

"Brother," he hesitated, "I counseled with a young Christian named Javier this morning, and he seemed quite confused."

"Yes, Brother Morgan, I know Javier. In fact, I also counseled him yesterday afternoon," I said.

"Yes, that's exactly why I wanted to talk to you," said the chaplain, "I'm concerned about some advice you gave Javier. As you know, he's been going through some real trials."

"Yes, I told him it's important that he do exactly what the Bible says for us to do, that he should 'give thanks in all circumstances,'[29] no matter how difficult things might be or how rough the situation," I said.

"That's the point," said Chaplain Morgan, "for you see Philip, Javier is not as mature a Christian as you are. He hasn't yet reached a level in his Christian walk where he is strong enough to do that. We have to remember, babies have to learn to crawl before learning to walk, and then it still may require some time before they can even run."

"Hmmm, I believe I catch your drift," I said. "Chaplain Morgan," I asked, "do you think my advice has caused Javier, and maybe other young Christians, to stumble?"

"No my brother, and don't you begin worrying," he smiled. "After all, we can't have you worrying. There's a whole lot of men that'll need your advice, and we need you singing! You can't sing if your heart's full of worry, now, can you?"

"No, you sure can't."

✞ ✞ ✞

On February 1, 1981, I visited my classification officer once again, only this time Chaplain Cornett went with me. After he had gone in before me to speak in my behalf, I was called in.

"Mr. Hicks," he began, "looking over your record I'll have to admit you've done extremely well while here. You've graduated from the Drug and Alcohol Abuse program, you have an excellent work record at the chapel, and you have made excellent grades in college. And, it's difficult to believe, but you haven't received a single bad report your entire incarceration. Hmmm, won't you step back outside the door for a moment? I need to talk with the sergeant once more."

As I sat on the hard wooden bench in the hallway, I thought to myself, surely they'll take at least two years off my parole date.

"Hicks, we're ready for you to come back in," echoed a voice from inside the office.

"Hicks, after careful consideration, I just don't see any real justification to make any changes on your date at this time.

However, we are going to request that your security status be lowered, from maximum to medium security," he finished.

"Thank you, Sir, thank you very much," I responded, as I hurriedly left.

Walking briskly back to my cell, I tried not to be disappointed. After all, I reminded myself, God knew just when I would be ready to leave. I also knew that there were a whole bunch of people who were now praying for me.

Stopping for a moment to tie one of my shoes, I saw something shiny in the grass reflected by the bright Florida sunshine. I reached over and picked it up—a single key attached to a solid ring. It was the inscription on the key that brought an instant smile.

On one side of the key were the words "ORAL ROBERTS' PRAYER ROOM," and on the flip side the words "TULSA, OKLA." and a telephone number, 918-495-7777. Beneath this was an engraving of the Prayer Tower, which is located on the campus of Oral Roberts University in Tulsa, Oklahoma. I had seen this while watching their program on television, and I also remembered that there were people up in that prayer tower, praying, 24 hours-a-day, 365 days a year.

Tightly grasping my new souvenir as I hurried back to show Vic what I had found, I was reminded that there were indeed many praying for me, and it didn't matter what the parole man said. After all, I was on a much higher time schedule.

Showing my key to Jess in the chapel library one afternoon, he said, "Yeah, they used to send those keys out to their ministry partners. I'll bet one of them was sent to a prisoner, who must've thrown it away."

"One man's trash is another man's treasure," I said excitedly.

Late one night Vic and I were in our cell. He was painting a portrait from a snapshot while I was trying to finish a letter before the guard brought the mail around.

"Feliciano," came a voice from the door as a bundle of letters was placed on the ledge of the small slit in our door.

"Well," I said, "not only did I not get this letter out, but you got all the mail tonight."

Since Vic's paints were lined across his bed I quickly got up and retrieved his mail.

"Hey Felipe," said Vic, "turn around ... you left a letter!"

"Now wait a minute. I know I got all the mail that was in that window!"

Reaching back to grab this mysterious envelope, I immediately lit up! "Hey! It's from my public defender at the West Palm Beach Court of Appeals! It's finally here!"

As I excitedly tore open the envelope, my heart began pounding ninety to nothin'! I read the letter aloud:

> Dear Mr. Hicks:
>
> I have now reviewed your transcript and file. I noticed your trial judge failed to read jury instructions although your attorney requested the same.
>
> The Florida Supreme Court has just recently ruled that as a reversible error, but the decision is not yet final. I am now waiting for their final decision before writing your brief since their decision will be controlling in your case.
>
> I am quite hopeful that you will then be given a new trial. Please rest assured your case is now being actively worked on, both by me and my associate, Ms. Denise Huard.
>
> You will be hearing from her just as soon as a decision has been reached.
>
> Sincerely,
> (Ms.) Cherry Grant
> Assistant Public Defender
> Fifteenth Judicial Circuit

"Praise the Lord!" Vic and I shouted almost simultaneously.

"Wow, Vic!" I shouted, "wouldn't this be something? This would be such a miracle!"

"What are you so excited about?" asked Victor, as he calmly brushed more paint on a landscape scene. "Felipe, you've been sayin' all along this was gonna happen, so why are you so surprised? You're always tellin' me, With God all things are possible."[30]

Looking over at my calm, cool, and collected Puerto Rican brother, I tried to act just as calm and real religious as I said, "Yes, my brother, our Father's promise *is* to set the captives free."

We both laughed as I just managed to dodge the pillow that was now flying past my head.

As soon as the nightly head count was finished and the doors were unlocked, I ran out of that cell and down the stairs to tell all the brothers the good news.

Two hours later I returned to find Vic fast asleep.

One of my favorite scripture passages is found in Jeremiah 29:11-14, which reads, "For I know the thoughts that I think toward you, says the Lord, thoughts of peace and not of evil, to give you a future and a hope. Then you will call upon Me and go and pray to Me, and I will listen to you. And you will seek Me and find Me, when you search for Me with all your heart. And I will be found by you, says the Lord, and I will bring you back from your captivity; I will gather you from all the nations and from all the places where I have driven you, says the Lord, and I will bring you to the place from which I caused you to be carried away captive."

God is not a respecter of persons and His promises are the same for all.

Just as He provided a single "door key" when I needed a reminder, it is who holds the keys to our destiny. We will walk in that promised destiny when we "seek Him" and "search for Him with of our hearts" and learn to be completely content regardless our circumstances.✝

Please rate the men's retreat:
(Circle one: Poor 1 2 3 4 5 excellent)

Meeting Facility:	1	2	3	4	5
Speakers:	1	2	3	4	5
Music:	1	2	3	4	5
Accommodations:	1	2	3	4	5

Please answer the following questions:

1. How did the retreat benefit you?

   ____

   ____

2. Were you blessed? In what way?

   ____

   ____

3. How will you implement what you learned at the retreat?

   ____

   ____

4. I am interested in attending the next retreat. Yes No

Comments:______________________________

____

____

Living Word Chapel
P.O. Box 91
Oracle, AZ 85623

LWC Men's Retreat Survey Card
Please fill out and mail back to church.

CHAPTER 23

NO PLACE LIKE HOME

While watching the Celtics blow out Atlanta on the tube one evening, someone tapped me on the shoulder. It was one of the guards.

"Hicks," he said, "you're wanted at the chapel."

"What's it about?" I asked.

"Don't know. Sarge just called inside and told us to send you over there. Here's your pass."

The door to Chaplain Shook's office was ajar, so I knocked and poked my head inside.

"Brother Shook," I questioned, "did you want to see me?"

Placing one hand on my shoulder he said, "Yes my brother, I've got some bad news for you."

"What is it?" I questioned, "Is … something wrong at home?"

"Yes, it's your younger brother Jerry. He was found dead at your parents' house today," replied Brother Shook.

"No … it can't be," I stammered. "How did it happen? How did it happen?" I questioned.

"At this time I don't know all the details, but I want you to talk to your parents," said Brother Shook. He dialed their number and handed the phone to me.

"Hello, Pop?" I asked a few seconds later. "Are you all right? Is Mother all right?"

I could hear both my parents' voices on the other end of the line, but I could hardly tell it was them. Considering all that they had been through with me, no doubt the shock of Jerry's death was too much for them to handle.

"Son," said Pop, "if it can be arranged, would you like to attend the funeral?"

"Well sure, Pop," I answered hastily, "but even if they'd let me go, don't you think it would be mighty rough on Mother? All her friends would see me with a guard and with handcuffs and all ... "

"Now, Son, don't you worry about that," interrupted Pop. "Your mother wants you to be here."

Chaplain Shook took the telephone receiver and gave Pop instructions on what to do so I could attend.

As they were talking, I said, "Excuse me, Brother Shook, would you please ask Pop to call Skip Nixon and ask if he could help arrange for a family friend to be deputized? He's a member of my folks' church and a former sheriff of Memphis. He's also served as Mayor of their county. If they could do that, I know it would be a lot better for my precious mother."

After giving Pop the instructions, Brother Shook hung up the phone and said, "Brother, let's pray about this situation."

At 6:00 A.M. two days later, I was sitting in a tiny holding cell, dressed in my prison blues, awaiting the arrival of the officer who would escort me to Memphis.

"Hicks, your ride is here," shouted the shift lieutenant. He unlocked the cell door and personally escorted me to the administration building.

"Open number three," came a voice over the intercom, followed by the loud thud of metal against metal as the iron-barred door slowly slid open.

I felt kind of strange as I walked through that door. Time had passed so quickly. I felt I had been at Raiford just a short while, yet more than eighteen months had already passed.

"Hello, Philip," said the tall, solidly built man standing with an officer at the outside control room.

Shaking his hand, I said, "Hello, Mr. Moore, it's real good to see you."

Smiling, he answered, "Yeah, I'll bet it is."

What happened next shocked the guards. They had already discovered Charles Moore wasn't even armed. But that wasn't the half of it.

"Aren't you going to handcuff him," demanded the control room sergeant, "and shackle him until you get him into your car?"

"No, I'm not," Mr. Moore calmly replied. "Thank you for your help and we'll see you in four days."

Mr. Moore was a real estate broker who attended my folks' church. I had known him since I was a child. As we traveled together, I learned that he had served as a volunteer deputy from time to time, but he was deputized specifically to escort me to and from Memphis.

I also learned that Mr. Moore had arrived at my parents' house right after Pop had spoken with Chaplain Shook. He had come over to pay his condolences. God had additional plans.

Before boarding our plane, Mr. Moore handed me some clothes and a pair of shoes. "Here," he said, "your brother, Dudley, bought these for you. Go into the restroom and change."

Five minutes later I walked out of that restroom dressed in a brand new suit. It fit perfectly, as did the brand new shoes. Now how did he know my size, I thought to myself.

During the flight home I brought Mr. Moore up to date on everything that had taken place in my life.

Afterwards he said, "Philip, I've known you since you were nine or ten years old. I've seen you and your brothers grow up. I've also known about your situation since you were sentenced. In fact, half the people at church have known about you. But since your mama is so embarrassed about your whereabouts, no one will bring it up. It's a shame, too, 'cause there's a whole lotta folks who've been waiting in the wings, wanting to console your parents. But they can't ... their hands are tied because they respect your parents so much.

"As you know, when the good Lord made your folks, He threw away the key. Not too many people are like your folks.

"Now Phil," he continued, "as you know, this is outside of regulations, but I'm gonna trust you and let you stay at your folks' house these three days. I only ask you to call me if you plan to go outside Shelby County while you're there, because I'd then need to accompany you in that case."

"How can I ever repay you?" I asked.

"Just make us proud, Philip, just make us proud," he replied.

On the morning of the funeral my sweet mother took me aside.

"Phil," she quietly said, "we would like you to speak today, but only if you feel comfortable about it. Jerry would have liked that."

"Sure, Mother," I said, "it would be an honor." I then gave her a strong hug and began softly praying for her.

That morning the funeral home was packed with well over three hundred people. Before I took my seat on the platform, I spoke to people I hadn't seen in years. There were guys with whom I used to ride motorcycles as well as those with whom I'd partied, folks from the church, former athletes from both my high school and Memphis State, and many who had attended school with me.

After the first preacher gave a short message, it was my turn to speak.

"Good morning," I began. "My family and I would like to deeply thank you for being here to support us. I can't tell you everything that has happened to me over the past few years, but I believe Jerry would have wanted me to tell you this. All my life I thought I was a Christian. I went to church. I tried to live right. I put money in the plate. Even sang in the choir some.

But the bottom line was, I only had "head knowledge" of the Lord versus knowing Him in my heart.

"I once heard a saying that went like this: 'Only nine inches separates a person from heaven and hell.' That's the approximate distance from a person's heart to his brain.

"But a little over two years ago some circumstances took place that resulted in my conversion experience. As my dad later said, 'Sometimes a man has to get knocked down in order to look up.' And yet, I'll never regret getting knocked down because as a result, I discovered an inner freedom and an inner joy that I'd never before known.

"My brother, Jerry, and I were very close. He probably understood me more than anyone else on the face of this earth. And after I got real with God, Jerry probably encouraged my Christian growth more than anyone else in my family. He did this by writing to me and reminding me of how much he believed in me, that he'd seen a change in me—even during his first visit with my parents.

"As many of you know, at the time of his death Jerry was married to his third wife, although he was only twenty-nine years old. His life was a mess and, quite frankly, he, too, had tried to find happiness in a lot of different things, but nothing seemed to satisfy.

"About a year ago," I continued, "I received a letter from Jerry. I'd like to read you parts of it."

> Dear Brother,
>
> I'm writing to tell you about some good news, which only you will be able to really appreciate. Recently I came home early from work. While sitting on my couch, I got real depressed. Suddenly I got the urge to get down on my knees and pray, something I don't recall ever doing. Phil, that day I gave my heart to God. I asked the Lord into my heart and before I got up from there I knew something had come over

me. It felt real good. I began going to church and even started reading my Bible. (I found my old Bible over at Mother and Pop's house, the Bible they had given me years ago when I joined the church.)

Phil, I even flushed all my grass down the commode. I quit looking at porn magazines, quit smoking, and even quit watching a lot of garbage on the boob tube. And you're not gonna believe this, but I've even stopped listening to a lot of hard rock music! I know people are gonna think all this is real strange, and that I've flipped, but you know, I don't care. Already, I feel so much better about myself.

I love you brother, and I'll be praying with and for you.

Your Brother ... in the flesh and in Christ, Jerry

"In case some of you didn't know, Jerry was one of the most talented musicians ever born in the city of Memphis. When he was younger, he played in a group with a couple of guys who have now made it big in the music industry. The reason I say this is, it had to be the grace and conviction of God for Jerry to be able to give up his hard rock music.

"And while I'm on this, Jerry's letter reminded me of something. As Christians, we're not supposed to be 'fruit inspectors.' In other words, it's not our job to go around telling others what Christians can or cannot do. Just like in Jerry's case, God did a real good job showing Jerry how Christians should live."

As I continued to talk, I sensed the Spirit of God on my words as His peace flooded my heart. The room was silent except for an occasional "Amen" or "Amen, Brother!"

Just as the Bible promises, I was given a "garment of praise for the spirit of heaviness"[31] that is always present at funerals.

"Anyway," I continued, "because my brother never experienced some necessary deliverance, some inner healing, and the power of God working in his life, his Christian walk resembled a roller coaster ride—up one day and down the next.

"I am confident, without a shadow of doubt, that my brother was called home early...by a loving, compassionate heavenly Father.

"And the same Father cares about every detail of your lives, too, just like He did Jerry's. This same Father wants each of you to experience the joy of Christianity, an ingredient my brother never really knew. But he sure wanted it, and today, he has it!

"Today, my brother has the victory. He's over all his problems and his tears have been wiped away. It is a day not to mope and be depressed, but a day to rejoice and be glad. Jerry is in heaven, and I know he'd like nothing more than for each one of us to one day join him. Let us pray."

✞ ✞ ✞

At my parents' home that afternoon, the kitchen overflowed with all types of delicious food. The house also overflowed with people of all walks of life.

That evening, after my parents had gone to sleep, I sat in the kitchen with my older brother and his wife, as well as a few friends. For hours they questioned me about the Bible and were shocked that I knew so much of it.

"Wild Man, you've really changed," said my old sound engineer buddy, Jerry Hadley. Jerry's friends called him "Friar Tuck."

People I used to run with used to call me nicknames such as Wild Man, Hyper Hicks, Fast Phil, among others, but it had been a long time since I had heard any of those names.

Someone said, "You've really changed."

"Oh, yeah. I definitely have," I acknowledged.

"Yes," said my cousin Dwight. "You've got a joy about you that you've never had before!"

"Philip, we're real proud of you," said my sister-in-law, Joanne.

"It's nothing I've done," I assured them. "The Lord is responsible for turning me into an entirely different person than the wild and crazy guy that y'all have always known."

For the next two days, several people who'd attended the funeral called me or dropped by to talk to me, asking questions like: "How can I get what you have?" or "How can I find the joy that you have?" or "Can you tell me more?"

Needless to say, several people came to know the Lord Jesus during this time, including Jerry's first and third wives, as well as my cousin Dwight. Later on, Dwight's wife wrote and said, "Dwight's selling his stock cars and has gone back to church!"

I was so glad to hear this. Not that there's anything wrong with having stock cars, as long as they don't come between you and God.

Before leaving to return to Raiford, I called the Memphis police lieutenant who had been put in charge of my being transported to Memphis. After thanking him for all his help, he assured me, "Well, Son, we were just glad we were able to help. However, you can be sure, if your record hadn't been as spotless as the people in Florida said it was, you'd have stayed in our county jail the whole time you were here. And you definitely would've been escorted to that funeral in shackles with an armed guard."

"God is good," I replied.

"Yes, son," said the lieutenant, "He certainly is. And He's always faithful to reward a person's diligence."[32]

After all the fantastic miracles that had taken place while in Memphis, I was actually looking forward to getting back to my "home away from home" so I could give a praise report of everything to my church between the fences.

Once again, I was laughing on the inside when I saw the shocked expression on the guards' faces when I was delivered by an unarmed officer.

I wonder if they realized how shocked I was when they didn't even frisk me before going back inside.

† † †

Once again, time sailed quickly by as my days stayed busy from dawn to dark. While I loved working at the chapel, I noticed many of my brothers in blue were being granted job transfers. So, I submitted a request to be transferred to the Outside Fence squad. Chances were my request would get shot down but there was no harm in asking. After all, James 4:2 says "you have not because you do not ask."

Meanwhile, God continued to give me favor with man, opening doors that most people would never believe. For example, following a visit, my dear Christian sister Joanne, the one who worked at a health food store and who had hired the attorney to represent me, wrote that she was concerned about my eating a balanced diet.

"Philip, I've written to the superintendent of the prison and asked permission to send you vitamins and protein powder. I'm now awaiting his answer," wrote Joanne.

Quite frankly, nobody was more surprised than I when one of the chaplains walked into my office one morning and said: "I've never seen anything like it, Brother Hicks. I was called to the Colonel's office this morning, and they've given you permission to receive this."

He then set a large sack on my desk. It contained three large cans of protein powder, in addition to several assorted containers of vitamins and minerals.

"Hmmm," he continued, "with all the drug problems on this compound, we don't wish to have the appearance of drugs. Maybe it'd be best if I keep most of this in my office, and you can feel free to pick up whatever you need, whenever you need it."

"No problem, Chaplain," I responded, "no problem at all!"

One night I received the miracle I'd been expecting. A letter from my public defender informed me my entire conviction had been vacated, based on the reversible error, and a new trial was scheduled for July 19. The letter also read:

> The State is offering you a plea bargain, in lieu of being re-tried. This plea bargain consists of the following:
>
> 1. You must plead "no contest"—meaning you're not pleading guilty or innocent.
> 2. The burglary charge will continue to stand, but the sentence will be changed from "life" to "ten years."
> 3. The possession of burglary tools charge will still stand, as well as the sentence of "five years."
>
> However, everything will now be run "concurrent"—meaning your sentence will now be a flat "ten years," instead of your present consecutive sentence of "life plus fifteen years."

"Victor," I excitedly screamed, "does this sound familiar to you?"

"What you mean, Felipe? How could it possibly be familiar to me?" he asked.

"Do you remember me telling you about that guy who was in the hospital with me at Lake Butler, the one who said he had worked in the law library? After looking at the list of errors that occurred during my trial, he told me that my sentence was a grudge sentence. He also said that in a couple of years, my case would be reversed and my sentence would be changed to ten years. Then they'd give me time served and let me go!"

"Glory to God, Felipe!" exclaimed Victor. "I do remember that. So, Felipe, you'd better pack your bags!"

This news set my feet to dancing, and that night, I don't think I slept a wink! It must've been dawn before I finally drifted to sleep, and I slept right through breakfast the next morning. Vic brought back some food, but it was a far cry from eggs or S.O.S.

I awoke to something icy cold on my chest. It was ice cream!

"Hey," I shouted. "Where did this come from?"

"Felipe," answered Vic, "the sergeant told me the Klondike Ice Cream Company had made a batch of these chocolate-covered ice cream bars, but the chocolate came out a darker color than what they advertised. So, they called the Department of Corrections and asked if they wanted it."

As I munched happily on a bar, I asked, "But why so many? You've brought me a dozen bars!"

"Yeah!" exclaimed Vic, "they're givin' out all you want, 'cause they don't have any freezer space left. They were donated—two tractor-trailer trucks full of the stuff!"

"Oh-h-h-h-h-h," I moaned, "there goes my waistline!"

"Man," said Vic, "you don't have to eat it."

"Yeah, I know, but these are my favorite ice cream bars, and besides, we never get ice cream!"

Guys were stuffing themselves with ice cream for days after that and getting sick right and left. But it wasn't only the humans who were getting sick. The seagulls were eating the leftovers—often entire boxes—and they were coming down with the worst case of seagull diarrhea that has surely ever been known. That stuff was flowing straight through those birds! For several days, the joint resembled a winter wonderland as the birds decorated the bushes all over the compound. Soon the guys were being sent to the Flat Top if caught feeding ice cream to the gulls!

In my public defender's letter, she advised me to either talk to a parole representative or to my classification officer before making a decision whether or not to accept the state's plea bargain offer. She also asked me to call her at her office, so I did that first.

"Yes, Brother Hicks," said Chaplain Cornett, "you may call her in my office. In fact, I'll charge the call to my credit card."

My P.D. told me the following: "If you choose to be retried, you'll probably lose, based on your previous confession, the available evidence, and, of course, the availability of witnesses."

"Yes, but didn't you say the guy who shot me, John Apostolou, is now under indictment by the Grand Jury for weapons charges?"

"Yes," she continued, "but he can still testify against you."

The next day, I asked my classification officer, "How will accepting the plea bargain affect my presumptive parole release date of 1986?"

"It won't," replied Mr. Williams. He went on to explain, "There'd be no effect because the Parole Board aggravated you on the charges of burglary and possession of burglary tools. These aggravations of nineteen months on each count would still be in effect, although the sentences would run concurrently."

After calling Denise Huard at the West Palm Beach Public Defender's Office and explaining what I'd discovered, she said she would ask the state attorney if he would agree to completely drop the possession of burglary tools charge.

"If he'll go for this," she explained, "this would, in turn, subtract nineteen months of aggravation from your presumptive parole release date (October 1986). Then, once your sentence is officially changed, Tallahassee will be notified, and they'll re-interview you. Most likely, they'll set you an earlier release date and send you to work release immediately."

"If they agree to that, I'll accept the plea bargain," I told her.

And she replied, "I had a strong feeling that you would."

The next day, my request for a job change was approved. After working at the chapel for over two wonderful years, I was assigned to the "outside fence" crew.

Had I known what was about to take place, I would have chosen to remain in the comfortable confines of my air-conditioned chapel office. Then again, maybe life had grown far too comfortable and it was time for my faith to be tried by fire.

After all, I'd been told, that's the only way to get refined.

Another favorite passage became effectual when I attended my brother's funeral. In 2 Corinthians 1:3-4, we're reminded that "the God of all comfort comforts us in all our affliction so that we may be able to comfort those who are in any affliction with the comfort with which we ourselves are comforted by God."

Most assuredly, our all-faithful Father empowered me with His supernatural comfort so I could comfort my precious parents, and so many others, throughout my visit in Memphis.

It is His desire to do the same for you.✝

CHAPTER 24

CLOSING IN ON THE OUTSIDE WORLD

The outside fence crew was responsible for a variety of jobs, including taking care of the lawns of high-ranking prison officials. Yet I heard it was a gravy assignment compared to the gun crew, where guys did road work under the supervision of guards armed with shotguns.

On my first day outside the fence, I met the sergeant in charge. I had already been filled in on him, as well as most of the other outside squad guards. Most of them had been brought up in this rural community where drinking beer, fishing, and hunting was their normal lifestyle. They all drove pickup trucks with shotgun racks above their seats. The word on them was that they were all rednecks who especially enjoyed their turn working the gun towers.

In other words, many of them disliked prisoners, and during an escape attempt they would shoot to kill an escapee.

Then again, they were all human beings who'd been raised no different than anyone else. God loved them all regardless of their way of life.

Our sarge stood about six-foot-tall, and he must have tilted the scales at around three hundred pounds. Of course, his weight varied with the size of his cud of chewing tobacco. I'd overheard that he'd been off work because his dad had recently passed away, and this was his first day back.

Surprisingly, he was very friendly, especially when I told him about my younger brother recently dying. He seemed interested in the events that surrounded my trip to Memphis, as well as learning about how I had come to know Christ.

Unfortunately, his friendliness didn't last long.

During my third week on the crew, I joined the other guys in taking a short break one afternoon. The temperature was around a hundred degrees that day, and we were using swing-blades to clear weeds around a nearby bridge.

"Hicks!" screamed the sergeant. "Did I tell you and Williams to take a break? Now git yore butts down in that ditch and finish up!"

Looking at the only other Christian on the crew, David Williams, I said, "But sarge ... " then I stopped short and said, "Yes, Sir!"

"In fact," said the sarge, "since Hicks and Williams were sluffin' off, everybody git back to work!"

"Give him no mind," said another inmate who was working alongside me, "that dude just don't like Christians. I heard him talkin' 'bout you before you left housing this morning. He wuz askin' Leonard if he thought you wuz fer real or not. Sarge thinks Christians are sissies. You'd better watch your back."

That night after chapel, I walked back to the housing area with Williams.

"Listen Philip," said Williams, "I've been on this crew a lot longer than you and have learned to ignore the sarge. We both know the only reason he does and says what he does is because he's unsaved. Besides, down underneath that brown uniform and three hundred pounds of tissue is a hurting little boy. He can't help it."

"Yeah, I know you're right," I said. "But it sure is disappointing. The guy was so open to learning about Jesus the first day we met. Now he's done a complete turnaround!"

"Well," said Williams, "you know what Leonard said—the sarge just don't like preachers or Christians. The Word encourages that everything we do, whether it be in word or in deed, we should do it unto the Lord. So, no matter what comes down, let's show them guys what we're made out of, OK? Whaddaya say?

As we both grinned and joined in a high five, I responded, "You got it brother! Let's do it!"

Incredibly, the most severe test of all was right around the bend.

✞ ✞ ✞

The next day was another burner. With the sun as hot as it was, I definitely didn't need any more heat. Then again, I kept remembering the Bible verse that says "when you walk through the fire, you shall not be burned."[33]

Our crew was working beside a two-lane highway picking up trash. We were all surprised when the sarge called another break, since we'd just finished lunch.

Williams and I walked to the pickup truck to get a refill of orange Kool-Aid® when Williams screamed, "Ow! A red ant just bit me!"

I couldn't help but laugh as he began slapping his leg. Only I was about to discover the truth about the old saying, "He who laughs last, laughs best," for I had been standing in the middle of a big patch of red ants, many of which were all over my shoes and heading northward.

I jumped up and down, screaming, "Ow-w-w-w-w-w! H-e-l-l-p-p! I'm covered with these things! They're in my underwear, too!"

As I hurriedly removed my pants, the laughter began. Here I was, standing out on the highway with my pants off, and wouldn't you know it, here came a car. But did I get any sympathy?

"*Hicks!*" yelled Sarge, "git them britches on, *now!*" But the sarge could hardly be mad, 'cause he, too, was bent over with laughter.

That afternoon we were chopping weeds on the edge of a big ditch. Because it had rained so much lately, the water had overflowed its banks and run up to a wooded area.

"Look at that moccasin!" said Jerome. He was pointing at a water moccasin, one of the region's deadliest snakes.

"Yeah," I said, "that's a big one." I didn't let on that I had always been afraid of snakes and was real glad that this one had glided across the water away from us.

"There's another one!" shouted Jerome.

I decided to move up to the area where Williams was working. It was a little further away from the water.

"Hicks! Williams!" screamed the sergeant. "Git out there in the middle of the water and chop them weeds that've grown up!"

Hesitatingly, I responded, "Uh, Sarge, isn't it a little deep out there?"

"Hell no," he said. "Now git out there ... now!"

"Sarge, there's water moccasins ... "

"Did you hear whut I said?" he demanded.

Williams and I tore out into the water, wildly swinging our blades as we screamed, "Praise the Lord! Praise the Lord! We bind these snakes in the name of Jesus! And we bind this fear, too!"

Soon every single weed was gone, but we just kept swingin' and screamin', enjoying that water to the max! Now two other guys ran into the water.

"I didn't say everybody!" yelled the sergeant. "C'mon, let's hit the truck."

After that day, Sarge let up on us.

✞ ✞ ✞

While the prison had employees who were unsaved, it also had staff who were Christians. It was common knowledge that one such person was old Mr. Jordan who ran the horticulture department.

Rumor had it Mr. Jordan had helped a whole bunch of former inmates, many of whom were now working in landscaping and ornamental horticulture out on the streets.

David Clark, one of my Christian brothers who was assigned to Mr. Jordan, invited me to visit his elderly boss with him one day.

After telling me all about their program and citing certain individuals who'd applied themselves while at Raiford and were now successful, I said, "Boy, I sure wish I could've taken the time to learn about flowers and plants while I've been here."

"Well, it's never too late," said Mr. Jordan.

"For me it probably is, because I'm a short timer now," I said. I brought Mr. Jordan up to date on everything that had happened.

"Where did you say you'd be going when you go back to court?" he asked.

"Fort Lauderdale, Sir," I responded. "To Broward County."

"And when are you going?" he asked.

"Any day now, Sir, any day," I said excitedly.

"Hmmm, have you ever heard of Jim Kizer?" he asked.

"No, sir, can't say that I have," I responded.

"Well," began Mr. Jordan, "Jim Kizer is a Jewish fellow who used to be in prison here. He had a pretty rough time of it, and one day he even tried to take his life. Didn't succeed, thankfully, and afterward I kinda took him under my wing and taught him the horticulture business. Got so good that when he transferred out to another prison, he was asked to go down to a new work release center in southern Florida where he personally designed and supervised the landscaping.

"When he got out, Jim was hired by Broward County for a program called Community Release. He works with inmates who are either on the way out of the system or who are already out. Goes to bat for them and helps them get a new start. I feel like Jim oughta know about you."

David couldn't have been more surprised than I when I was handed the telephone receiver a few minutes later and a voice on the other end of the line said, "Philip, Jim Kizer here. How can I help you?"

Twenty minutes later I had answered several questions and Jim said, "As soon as you arrive here at the county jail, tell the officers you need to speak to me."

"Yes, sir," I said, "I'll sure do just that. Thank you, thank you very much."

"Don't thank me," he said, "Thank Mr. Jordan. That man did so much for me; the least I can do is try to help others as best I can."

In a day and age when Christians are being tortured and even killed just because they are Christians, I had very little to complain about while enduring red ants, water moccasins, and a redneck sergeant who seemed to go out of his way to antagonize believers. After all, since the Church began Christians have been tortured and killed. The example of Paul and Silas being tortured and humiliated in the nineteenth chapter of Acts paints a vivid picture of persecution in the early Church. And how did they respond? When they took their eyes off themselves and their circumstances and began to praise God and sing songs unto Him in the midst of their ordeal, an all-knowing, all-powerful heavenly Father caused an earthquake to bring

them freedom! When their jailer saw their joy, he too wanted to be saved! Every believer is being watched by unbelievers who are still searching. One of our greatest forms of witness is to praise God in things so others can see and, prayerfully, believe.

When challenges and disappointments seem unbearable, I encourage you to take your eyes off yourself and consider others who have experienced far worse difficulties, even death, because of their beliefs.✞

CHAPTER 25

SHORT TIMER

While volunteering in the chapel late one Saturday afternoon, there was a knock on the door.

"C'mon in," I said.

"Hey, Brother!" said another chapel aide. "I've got some great news for you."

"Hello, Nat, what's the good word?" I asked.

"The transfer list is out, and you're on it!" he said.

"What? You mean I'm getting moved to another joint?"

"Well, not exactly," he explained. "You see, on the bottom of the transfer list is the list of guys who'll be leaving for outside court, and you're on it! Monday morning, you're outta here!"

After letting out a war whoop that was probably heard across the street in the visiting park, I charged out of the office and down the hallway. I couldn't wait to tell the chaplains the good news.

As it turned out, they already knew. In fact, I was the last to know.

Since it was only Friday, I had until Monday morning to write and call people and ask them to keep me in their prayers.

That night I wrote Phoebe a quick note.

Dearest Sister Phoebe,

Grace to you, and peace from God the Father and the Lord Jesus Christ! I hope this finds your heart filled with joy unspeakable ... mine sure is! Guess what??? I'll be in Fort Lauderdale next week, and should arrive by Wednesday. I sure am looking forward to seeing you, and as many of our brothers and sisters that can visit me while I'm there in the County Jail. As I previously stated, they've set my trial date for July 19. Of course, since I'm going to accept the state's plea bargain, I won't be re-tried. However, I would sincerely appreciate your calling my new public defender, Denise Huard, and asking her approximately how long I will be in Fort Lauderdale, and if it's only for two or three days, can the Public Defender's Office arrange for me to receive extra visits since my physical condition prevented my receiving regular visitors last time?

Thank you, Phoebe! See you here, there, or in the air!

In Christ's love, Philip

✟ ✟ ✟

I don't know about the other guys, but I felt a little like a sardine must feel, wedged in the back of the van for the trip south two days later. But I didn't mind it one bit. In fact, I wasn't even bothered by the shackles that held my wrists together nor the irons attached to my ankles.

That first day we made several stops at other prisons to drop off and pick up prisoners. We spent Monday night at a County Jail near Daytona Beach. Well, for part of a night anyway, as we were back in the van at 4:00 A.M. the next morning.

Tuesday proved to be a repeat of Monday, only it was between 4:00 and 5:00 A.M. the next morning before we pulled into the garage of the Broward County Jail.

I couldn't have been more surprised the moment I got out of the van. As we waited on the guard to unlock the rear door, I noticed another vehicle pull into the garage and park beside our van. Its driver got out about the very same time that I did, and our eyes met. We both smiled.

"Well, Praise the Lord!" I shouted.

"Hello, Brother," exclaimed Officer Rex. "I saw your name on the incoming transportation list, and I knew the Lord had worked a miracle in your life!"

"What are you doing here?" I asked.

"Well," he said, "ordinarily I don't work tonight, but they called me to do overtime. I left duty inside almost two years ago, about the time you were at the jail in your body cast, and I switched to transportation."

"Brother Rex," I said, "I'll never forget how you picked up that long extension cord and arranged it so I could make telephone calls from the back of my cell. Praise the Lord, you're such a servant!"

"Our Lord led by example and so should we," Brother Rex responded, as he raised his hand to give me a high five. Quickly raising my hand to slap his hand, I completely forgot about my shackles!

"Ouch!" I yelled, as we both laughed.

"Watch it feller, or they'll have you back in the hospital!" he said, and we laughed again. "I'll come by and talk with you after they process you," he said. He then turned to unlock his own van full of transfers.

After sitting in a holding cell for more than an hour, I was startled when my name was called.

"Hicks," said a guard at the cell door. "Wake up; it's your turn to be processed."

"I'm right here," I responded.

"Follow me," directed the officer.

As I stepped up to the window where an officer fills out forms on the new men, I noticed the clock on the wall. It was five minutes after six.

"Sir," I asked, "what time does Jim Kizer arrive?"

"Jim who?" asked the officer.

"Uh, Jim Kizer," I answered. "He told me to ask for him. He works for the Broward County Sheriff's Department, for Community Release.

"Never heard of him," said the officer.

"Well," I continued, "do you mind asking someone else? I'm confident he works here."

With an arrogant expression on his face the officer turned around and half-heartedly asked, "Has anyone ever heard of a guy name Jim Kizer?"

Across the room, an officer sitting behind a desk responded, "Yes, that's Kizer walking through the door right now. Hey, Jim, they want to see you at the window!"

I couldn't have been more relieved when this slim, distinguished fellow with grey hair, dressed in a three-piece suit, walked over to the window and said, "Excuse me, officer."

When the officer stepped aside, Jim Kizer extended his hand and said, "Hello, Philip, as soon as you're through here, I'll visit with you."

As it turned out, he had to wait his turn, as shortly afterward Officer Rex told a guard to let me out of the holding cell again.

"Hungry?" he asked as he handed me a cup of coffee along with the most delicious looking donut I'd ever seen. It just dawned on me that I hadn't eaten since late afternoon the day before, and there's just something about one slice of bologna on two pieces of white bread that doesn't keep a man filled for long. Don't get me wrong, I was thankful for the sack lunch they had prepared for our trip; I was just too excited to eat much of it.

After I spent close to an hour bringing Officer Rex up on all that had taken place, it was Jim's turn to get acquainted.

"I've done some research on the guy who shot you," he began, "and man, you were involved with some heavy company, whether you knew it or not. He's got a record of arrests that's as long as your arm, but ironically all his charges were always dropped. I'm not talking about petty stuff. Charges like possession of heavy weapons, assault on a police officer, possession of controlled substances, and intent. Makes one think the fellow may have been working both sides of the fence. But no matter, what goes around comes around, and his lifestyle has evidently now caught up with him. He's under indictment by the Grand Jury, and this time he's going to catch some time."

"Seems ironic," I said, "that about the time I'm on the way out, he may be on the way in. And if he is a snitch, he won't last long in the joint!"

"That is an understatement my friend," added Jim. "But now," he continued, "let's talk about you. I've already talked to the judge who you'll go before to accept the plea bargain. Also, there are some of your friends who want to speak on your behalf. We're going to ask the judge if he'll order an immediate transfer for you—down to a work release center in this area. So keep it in prayer, and God's will be done."

"Sounds good to me," I said, "but no matter what happens, I sure appreciate everything you've done."

"Glad to help," Jim added as he walked me back to the holding cell.

Back in my cell, I thought about my conversation with Jim as we discussed the possibility of John going to prison.

"Lord," I silently prayed, "please forgive me for judging John. Far be it from me to throw stones or judge another. After all, it's Your will that all be saved and perhaps You are already preparing his heart to cry out and receive You, just as I cried out in my trouble. I ask You to even now open John's heart and give him faith to believe in You. Go before him, and send laborers across his path. In Jesus' name I pray and thank You. Amen."

After four wonderful days of getting to see many of my friends, I was returned to Raiford. Only this time, I wasn't carrying a consecutive life plus fifteen years on my back.

Now I had a brand new ten-year sentence, and as the guys in the joint might say, I could do that standin' on my head.

But, deep within, I knew I was a short-timer.

In Matthew 5:44-47 Jesus commands us to "Love your enemies, bless those who curse you, do good to those who hate you, and pray for those who spitefully use you and persecute you, that you may be sons of your Father in heaven; for He makes the sun rise on the evil and on the good, and sends rain on the just and on the unjust. For if you love those who love you, what reward have you? Do not even the tax collectors do the same?"

It's impossible to love and forgive in our own strengths, but with God's help we can walk in obedience. When we walk in obedience, we will no longer have spite in our hearts toward others. God will not ask us to do something that Jesus didn't do Himself. As He hung dying on a cross His powerful words said it all: "Father, forgive them for they know not what they do."

Perhaps you are harboring unforgiveness in your heart toward your wife, ex-wife, or children? Perhaps your parents hurt you? Perhaps your homey snitched you out, and you've never forgiven him? Do you hold a grudge, resentment, and bitterness toward the judge who sentenced you?

I encourage you to ask God to give you the strength and courage to forgive others, and He will! Now, ask Him to give you His power to love your enemies and pray for them, that God will even send the rain of His love upon them. He will! This will set your heart free, and your heavenly Father will send much grace into your life.✞

CHAPTER 26

DECONTAMINATION CHAMBER

After returning to Raiford, I found they had assigned my bunk to someone else. On one hand it was a real bummer because roommates like Victor were hard to find. But on the other hand, I knew I wouldn't be there much longer. By this time I had learned to adapt in any situation.

When I found out Vic's new roommate was Hispanic, and a young Christian to boot, I could already see God's hand in all this. I had been encouraging Vic for over a year, and now it was his turn to pass it on. Quite frankly, though, it was Vic who had been doing much of the encouraging. That's the way I saw it from my side of the room, so to speak.

My new job assignment was working outside the prison as a clerk at the motor pool. It was a nearly perfect position. My boss was a Christian, and as long as I got my work done, he didn't mind me leaving my desk to work out with weights, sit out under the spacious skies watching the sea gulls flying overhead, have devotions, write letters, or whatever.

At times I felt like I was already free. That is, until it was time to walk back across the road and re-enter the prison at 5:00 P.M. each evening.

"All right," said the guard as we walked through the gate one evening, "everybody up against the wall. It's shakedown time."

I had grown accustomed to being checked for contraband each night after work. Inmates would often be caught smuggling in grass and even beer, which they'd bought from guards or free men who worked at the motor pool or meat processing plant. At the latter, inmates were used to help slaughter all the chickens, pigs, and cows that would eventually be fed to the inmates. (Only one problem: For some reason we saw steak only twice a year, including our annual Christmas meal.)

"Check this out!" exclaimed a laughing inmate after we'd returned to the housing area one night.

Assigned to the meat plant, he had wrapped sirloin around his biceps and got past the guards when he was frisked. The majority of inmates pumped iron when they hit the joint, and most would make good candidates for Muscle Magazine. It wasn't difficult to get past the guards with stolen beef wrapped around their biceps. Inmates were experts at smuggling in contraband.

"Fantastic!" shouted his roommate, "we're gonna eat good tonight!"

"Yeah," responded the prisoner with the steak. "Better us than them. Everybody knows them guards got iceboxes full of meat at home."

A week later all the guys assigned to the motor pool were called to the office for a meeting.

"Listen," said the sergeant, "they've decided to ship this entire crew over to the Old Unit to make more room for new arrivals. We're getting overcrowded again, and the last thing we want is another inmate riot at the Rock. So, when you leave work today, go straight to your cells, get your gear, and report back to the gate immediately."

"But Sarge," complained one guy, "I don't wanna go over there. I likes it fine where I am ... "

"No buts about it," interrupted the sergeant, "ain't nothin' I can do about it. These are orders from the top."

On the way back inside I turned to Larry, the only other professing Christian assigned to the Motor Pool, and said, "Man, I don't see why that guy would turn down going to the Old Unit. I hear that's nothing but easy livin' over there."

"That's simple," said Larry, "the dude lives with his girl at the Rock, and he sure don't want to lose his romance. Besides, I hear he does all right at selling dope too."

"Oh, now I get the picture," I answered.

"Yeah, everybody's got their own thing," added Larry. "Philip, I'm a little nervous about going over there. Well, you see, I'm scheduled to leave soon, and I don't want to do anything stupid that'll mess up my release. It's just that I miss my wife and children so much. That open gate would be such a temptation."

"Now, Larry, you're gonna' be just fine," I assured him. "Tell you what, let's agree in prayer that we'll get to be roommates. That way, we can encourage each other, the time will fly by, and you'll be going home before you know it."

A person can still see Raiford from the Old Unit. Located across a big field, this minimum security prison is also found across the road from still another joint, Florida State Prison. I discovered the Old Unit to be a real sweet camp. It didn't have gun towers but a single short fence, and its only gate was always left standing wide open.

We hadn't been there one hour when I leaned back in a chair and exclaimed to Larry, "Man, it's so great to be trusted again." We also noticed there was a different spirit about that place.

"Hicks," said the officer in charge, "you're assigned to cell 2T."

"Uh, sarge," I said, "could I request a certain roommate?"

"Sorry, Hicks," answered the sergeant, as he glanced at a computer printout, "there's already someone assigned to your cell. Hmmm, his name is Gooddall, Larry Gooddall."

"Well, Praise the Lord," I said. I whirled around and exchanged a high five with Larry as we headed down to find our new quarters. "God's done it again."

On the way I stopped at the linen room to pick up my sheets.

"You're a Christian, aren't you?" asked a young inmate, as he handed me my packet of linens.

I grinned and asked, "How'd you know?"

"Man, I can see it all over you," answered the inmate, who introduced himself as Michael.

"I guess that's the greatest compliment I've ever had," I told my new brother.

Joining Larry and me at our dinner table that evening, we learned more about Michael. And again, I was reminded of how small the world really was, especially when Christians began covering it.

It turned out that not only was Michael from Fort Lauderdale, but he had become a Christian in the Broward County Jail. The preacher who led Michael to salvation was none other than James "Butch" Ridgway at the Potter's House. It was good ol' faithful Charlie Heinline who'd encouraged his scripture study through the Navigators' memorization work. Charlie was the same brother who'd encouraged me to memorize scripture when he visited me in the very same county jail.

That night I wrote Phoebe.

> Dearest Sister Phoebe,
>
> I have been moved to my "Judea," and this place is as different as night and day compared to my "Jerusalem" over at U.C.I. This is no prison; this is like a Boy Scout camp, and it surely serves as my decontamination chamber, a place to prepare me for my upcoming re-entry into society!
>
> Alleluia! The atmosphere is so relaxing. There's no tension like at U.C.I., because the men here all have short

sentences! If only they knew, yours truly now has the shortest sentence of all!! Glory to God!

Phoebe, the meals here are delicious and HOT, as the cooks take pride in their work. In fact, the guys get to choose where they want to work! We get steak and lobster – every meal! Just kidding, but we do have a separate salad bar, and we even get to choose what kind of dressing we want! And, each cell has its own private shower! And Phoebe ... each cell has its own private back porch, with a door on it! It's fantastic, I can go out there at night, look up at the stars and sing praises to our King of Kings and Lord of Lords!!! My own private prayer room, even better than my "Mount of Olives" over on the hill overlooking the Motor Pool! Alleluia!

While I sure miss all our brothers over at UCI, the church here is fifty strong, and their chaplain, Austin Brown, is an ex-lifer who became a chaplain after being paroled! He's sure got a heart for God!!

I'll close for now, but always remain with you in spirit and in prayer. Have a beautiful week ... go out and collect all He has prepared especially for you. I love you abundantly!!

Philip

In the first chapter of Acts, verse 8 reads "You shall receive power when the Holy Spirit has come upon you; and you shall be My witnesses both in Jerusalem, and in all Judea and Samaria, and even to the remotest part of the earth."

While being moved from cell to cell, from job to job, and from facility to facility, it became apparent that this was all part of my heavenly Father's plan—that I would be

His witness to hurting people who, like me, needed a relationship with Him.

All He requires is a surrendered life through whom He can touch and encourage others.

He is calling you for this divine purpose, and as soon as you take your eyes off yourself and your circumstances, and look to help someone else in need, you're going to see your life change in remarkable ways!✞

CHAPTER 27

A NEW BEGINNING

It's been said that "all good things must come to an end," but I was probably the most surprised when, after five wonderful days at the Old Unit, our entire squad was moved back to UCI.

"How come we were returned?" I asked my Motor Pool supervisor one morning after we'd been back a couple days.

"Well," he said, "the time was too easy for a couple of the guys. They just couldn't adjust, not to mention the word is they were heavy escape risks."

"Well then," I questioned, "why in the world were we moved in the first place, since they knew about all our records?"

"That's the Administration for you," he said before walking away.

Fortunately for me, I had no way of knowing that during my final two months at Raiford, I would live in six different cells, in three different housing areas.

My favorite place turned out to be at the Main Unit, the oldest area on the compound. Also called "the Rock," its recreation yard included a football field as well as concrete walls where the guys could play handball. Rumor had it the State had condemned this unit due to inhumane living conditions, but political red tape kept it opened until additional housing units could be built elsewhere.

My different roommates included a man who everybody thought was a Christian, but who was really playing games behind closed doors. I was reminded that there will always be "tares among the wheat."[34] This was such a valuable lesson as both people on the streets and behind the wall often use "the hypocrites" as their justification to not go to church, saying "that church is filled with phonies." And yet, even Jesus in the parable of the tares and wheat warned us that there will always be hypocrites in church, but don't let them prevent us from seeking the Lord! They'll always be there and they'll get their reward in the end.

And speaking of "bad," another Christian was named Bernie DeCastro. Standing about six foot two inches and weighing around 225, Bernie looked like he could set any weightlifting record and yet, he was as gentle as a lamb. Bernie had been sentenced from Miami, Florida, for multiple counts of armed robbery and was serving a life plus thirty years sentence. He was one of the toughest guys around until he met Jesus and allowed Him to transform his life! Yes, Jesus showed Bernie what it takes to be a real man ... that is, to lay aside his own reputation and put the needs of others first. One of the remarkable things I remember about Bernie was that he had been appealing his sentences for about five years before he met Jesus. He figured that there were only three ways that he was ever going to get out of prison—the appeals court, over or under the fences, or in a pine box. Having been tried, convicted, and sentenced, parole was not an option for Bernie. Well, after Bernie met Jesus, he was led to abandon his appeals and put his complete trust in God's promises to "open wide the prison gates." So, one day he tore up all of his legal papers—two boxes of them—and said that he was through trying to manipulate the system.

According to Bernie, "I'm guilty of the crime I'm sentenced for, and if Jesus wants me out then He can do it His way.

Approximately two years later, Bernie was miraculously paroled and later received a full and unconditional pardon from the Governor of Florida!

One day Bernie came to me with a special request.

"Brother Phil, we're trying to find a mature Christian to move in with Richie, and the brothers have decided you're about the only guy who could handle him. Whaddaya say?"

Bernie had taken on a real burden for Richie. The word was out that Richie was possessed with schizophrenic personalities. The kid wanted to do right but his other personalities were too much for him to handle.

In the end, I agreed to move in with him, which really flipped out the sergeant who was in charge of that housing area—he'd never found anyone who could live with Richie for over a week. If I hadn't been praying, as well as many others who were fasting for the situation, I couldn't have lasted as long as I did, either.

One night I was awakened by a kind of growling noise. Turning over, I found Richie standing at the foot of my bed, saying, "I am the devil! You are going to die!"

For a moment, a spirit of fear came over me; but then I rose up, and with a low but firm voice I said, "I rebuke and bind you in the name of Jesus!"[35]

Afterward Richie—rather the other person speaking through him—didn't say anything. He just stood and stared.

So I finally got up the courage to roll over, close my eyes, and drift off to sleep. And yet, you can believe that I was doing some heavy praying in the Spirit as I fell asleep.

I awoke the next morning to find Richie shaking my bed and saying, "Wake up, Brother! You're gonna miss breakfast ... and they're serving your favorite, pancakes!"

Jumping out of bed I hurriedly dressed, and we headed out the door. On the way I turned to Richie and asked, "Richie, do you remember standing up and shouting anything last night?"

"What in the world are you talking about?" demanded Richie. "You must have had a bad dream! Must've been the pizza we had for chow."

"Yeah, it must've been the pizza," I shouted, as I jumped into a sprint. "C'mon, I'll race you to breakfast!"

✞ ✞ ✞

It saddened me to see Richie check himself into the Annex less than a week later. The Annex was part of the prison hospital where the inmates with mental and emotional problems were housed. The saddest part was that most of them were kept zonked out on Thorazine, and very few ever got better. I never saw Richie again.

Many Christian groups regularly came off the street to minister at Raiford. Included in these groups was an interdenominational program called Cursillo. Actually, that was the name of their organization on the street, but their prison outreach had the label of Kairos. This dedicated group of preachers, priests, and volunteers held three-day retreats at Raiford, as well as at other prisons, at least twice a year.

The inmate participants were randomly selected, and once a person attended the retreats, he was eligible to attend the monthly meetings, called Ultreyas. These retreats were very special. In addition to the informal speakers, rap sessions, and eating all our meals with our Christian brothers from outside the fence, Christians from all over the world were praying for our special weekend.

Throughout the retreat, home-cooked meals were prepared and delivered to us, as well as delicious homemade cookies, a bowl of which was kept full on each table throughout the retreat.

On the final day, each attending inmate received a sackful of cards, written especially to them from Christians from all over the United States. The inmates got to take the cards back to their cells, in addition to sacks and sacks of homemade cookies, which were shared with the guys in their buildings.

During the monthly Ultreya reunions, a time was set apart for guys to give testimony to what God was doing in their lives. On one particular Sunday, a young Christian brother named Robert stood up to testify.

"Last Tuesday night," said Bobby, "God healed my leg. I was born with one leg shorter than the other. But last Tuesday, Brother Smith preached at our Bible Study."

I turned to the inmate sitting next to me and whispered, "Who's Brother Smith? What's that about?"

"Brother Smith is a Citizen Volunteer. He teaches a weekly Bible Study on Tuesday nights."

"Oh," I said.

"At the end, he asked if anyone wanted prayer for physical healing," Bobby continued. "I went forward, and they took me back into the chaplain's office. They had me sit on a chair, and began to pray for me. Ten minutes later, my leg had grown out almost three inches!!"

Suddenly the whole place went wild, as a chorus of "Praise the Lord!" rang out from virtually every pew.

Well, as Bobby told this, the Holy Spirit spoke to me and said, "Philip, it's time you used your faith to pray for specific healing for your leg."

That night, I decided that I was going to go see Brother Smith the next week. While having devotions the next morning out at the Motor Pool, the thought came to mind once again.

I was surprised when a tall, thin man walked through the door of my little clerk's office, someone who seldom came outside the fence while on duty.

"Chaplain Shook!" I cried, and instantly I knew that I didn't have to wait on any person in particular, such as Brother Smith. As long as I had the faith, joined with the person doing the praying, God would heal my leg, too.

"Chaplain Shook," I exclaimed again, "God wants to heal my leg. Would you please pray for me?"

Grinning from ear to ear, Brother Shook said, "Well, I thought you were never going to ask! As I recall, it's been several months since your doctor showed you an x-ray of your femur, Philip."

"Yes. And even the doctor was amazed at how perfectly the bone had healed. However, my right leg is visibly almost two inches shorter than the other."

"It's time, Brother. Let us begin." Chaplain Shook took my hand as I sat up in my folding chair. He then held my legs out straight and began praying.

We both began praying in the Spirit,[36] thanking Jesus for taking stripes on his body for our healing.

I sensed an awesome presence in the room as Brother Shook excitedly exclaimed, "It's grown about one-fourth of an inch ... now one-half ... Glory to God ... Praise you Jesus ... all right, that's over an inch ... only about one-half inch to go now! It's done!"

I jumped up and hugged Brother Shook. I couldn't wait to tell someone.

After Brother Shook left, I ran outside and the first person I saw was my supervisor, a free man who someone had told me belonged to a local Baptist Church.

"Guess what?" I exclaimed.

"What is it now, Hicks?" he asked.

"God just healed my leg! Brother Shook ... "

"Now, Hicks," he interrupted, "there's a guy over at your parts window, waiting for a part ... "

"Yes, Sir," I quickly said, "on the double!"

Actually, I wasn't that surprised by the man's reaction. By now I had learned some Christians believed in the entire Bible, whereas others, regardless whether they were Baptists, Methodists, or whatever, believed some of God's promises had already passed away.

Yet no matter what a person believed or didn't believe, I was growing to respect people for just being people. They had a right to believe whatever they wanted to believe.

Speaking for myself though, I truly believed the whole Bible was still in effect. "Jesus Christ—the same yesterday, today, and forever!"[37]

That night I went to visit my old roommate, Victor, and you should have seen the reaction on his face when I sat down on the floor and showed him my leg.

"Vic, look ... God healed my leg!" I said. While exercising with Vic for well over a year, he had noticed the shortness of my leg, but he didn't want to say anything and hurt my feelings.

"Glory a Dios! Razando al Senor!" he exclaimed.

"Isn't it wonderful?" I shouted.

"Felipe," he continued, "your leg, it's the same length as the other one! This is fantastic! How did it happen?"

I tried to be cool, as I calmly said, "Well Hermano, our Father didn't want me leaving prison until I was completely restored ... in spirit, soul, and body!"

"Be cool now," he laughed and said, "before I have to humble you by breaking your other leg!"

Three weeks later Chaplain Shook asked me if I wanted to deliver a short message during the morning service. Ironically, it was the day before I left Union Correctional Institution at Raiford, Florida.

That night I found it difficult to fall asleep. I was still crying when I finally began dreaming. The last thing I remember praying was, "Oh God, my heart hurts so much because I'm really going to miss my brothers in blue."

After arriving at Pompano Correctional Center in Fort Lauderdale less than two days later, I was assigned to take care of the Visiting Park. It was located next to the chapel, and it was filled with beautiful trees and flowers. I worked at the Center until my time was short enough to qualify for work release.

"Oh, so you're another one of those Jesus freaks," said Mr. Smith, the sergeant in charge of the Center's work assignments. "Then you won't mind keeping the chapel clean during your spare time, now will you?" he asked.

"Why no, sir," I responded, "I'll be glad to do that." I couldn't help but hear him snickering as he quickly walked away.

"Hey, Mr. Smith," I called, "one more thing. I hear they don't have any programs for the young people when they come out here on Sundays to visit with their parents. Well, Sir, one of the things I did up at Raiford was help with the weekly children's Sunday school class. I'd sure like to start one here. In fact, I once worked as a clown out in Colorado. I have a lot of ideas for a program."

"Sure Hicks," he said, "we'll give you a shot, but keep it on the level, you hear, or you'll be getting up at 4:00 A.M. and working in the kitchen."

From my first day at Pompano C.C., friends from just about every type of church in the Fort Lauderdale area began calling to ask if they could visit me. Due to regulations, our visiting lists were limited, but once again I was given favor by the prison officials.

During an afternoon visit with Brother John Harber, his daughter Jane, and her husband Rich Moore, we discussed this.

"I'm so surprised they bend the rules so much for me," I said.

"Well," said Rich, "scripture says that as God's children we will be given favor with man."

"Yeah," I answered, "but doesn't that mean favor with Christians?"

"No, Brother," interjected Jane, "it promises we will be given favor with all men, regardless if they're saved or not."[38] A former prayer coordinator for Dwight Thompson Ministries, Jane had overcome some heavy obstacles of her own en route to becoming one of the strongest Christians around. And she was the perfect support and helpmate for Rich, who was quickly becoming a noted Bible teacher.

Rich had come a long way from playing professional basketball, before turning to the business world and the bottle to try to fill up the emptiness within his soul.

"Speaking of visiting lists," said John, "there's a young lady on the staff at our church who I think you should meet. Her name is Dewella. She's the best ventriloquist I've ever seen, and if you'd invite her, I bet she'd come out here and do a program for the children some Sunday."

"Well, John," I said, "anybody you recommend is bound to be special. I'll be glad to call her."

The next Friday I was vacuuming the chapel when I heard my name being called over the loud speaker. "Hicks, you have a visitor. Hicks, you have a visitor in the office."

Oh wow, I thought, and I'm covered with dirt from working in the Visiting Park. As I ran out of the chapel I almost tripped over the broom I'd left on the porch. Grabbing it on the run, I dashed across the lot and entered the side door to the office.

A very pretty girl with dark hair immediately stuck out her hand and said, "I'm Dewella, you must be Philip."

"Well, Praise the Lord, Sister," I responded, "I'm pleased to meet you. Would you like to walk over and see our chapel? We can talk about the Sunday School class over there."

The next Sunday morning, not only did God anoint my new friend to keep the children on the edge of their seats, but she kept the adults rolling in the aisles, too. Well, that is, her dummy, Oscar, did. Of course, she had a little something to do with it.

As the weeks passed, Dewella and I combined our ministry outreach, and before long we were getting invitations to visit nearby churches, a local mission, and a high school. In fact, for three weeks straight, I was off the compound no less than five nights a week.

"Boy, Hicks," said a fellow inmate named Bob Brown one afternoon, "they might as well release you. After all, you're never here."

Speaking of release, one morning my classification officer came to see me. Coincidentally, Brother John Harber had just stopped by to bring me a big sack of fresh fruit and a quart of fresh-squeezed Florida orange juice. She allowed him to sit in on our meeting.

"After considering your sentence and looking over your record, I'm going to recommend they change your presumptive parole release date from October, 1986 to August 23, 1985."

"But Miss Alexander," I said, "my sentence was changed from life plus fifteen years to ten years, and they told me that by dropping the possession of burglary tools it would subtract ninteen months from the 1986 date immediately, not to mention my spotless record ... "

"Now Mr. Hicks," she interrupted, "there are guidelines we have to follow. The Parole Commission will make a final decision in one month. I might add that they allow family and friends to speak on behalf of the men and women whose cases they're deciding."

"What about me? Do I get to speak to the Parole Commission, too?" I asked.

"No, I'm afraid not," she replied.

For a second I had to fight back a big lump in my throat, but somehow I was able to say, "Thank you, Miss Alexander. I know you have your guidelines."

A short time later I walked John to his car. After giving me a big hug good-bye, Brother John said, "Philip, you've heard the song that goes something like, 'He wouldn't bring us this far to leave us,' haven't you?"

Looking up at him I returned his grin and said, "You are so right, and besides this Center is another mission field in itself, and I'll get out when I'm ready and not a day before. After all, God's time schedule is always perfect! Amen?"

"That's the Philip I know!" said John.

Throughout the afternoon I stayed busy raking leaves out in the Visiting Park. And for some reason I kept singing that song, over and over again. "He wouldn't bring us this far to leave us. Ba-bu-ba-bu-ba. He wouldn't build us up to let us down. Do ... Do ... Do ... Do ... Do. He wouldn't build his home in us-s-s-s, to move a-w-a-a-y. He wouldn't lift us up, to let us d-o-w-n-n- n-n."

That night, I went to sleep hummin' that song.

The following week they let me go on work release, and once again my path was ordered. A friend from John's church owned a plastering company, and he hired me.

It was rough hard work, mixing mud out in the hot Florida sun before rolling mud-filled wheelbarrows to the plasterers. But I loved every single minute of it.

One day after chapel I was sharing a picnic lunch with Dewella. "The Lord is leading me to begin a twenty-one-day fast on your behalf," she said.

"What!" I exclaimed. "You'll starve to death. I don't want you to do that."

"Philip, it's not a matter of what you want," she continued. "When God directs a person to do something, it's important that we're obedient. Now some other brothers and sisters are going to be joining me, at least for partial fasts. Your parole hearing in Tallahassee is coming up soon, and we believe it's going to take much prayer and fasting to turn the hearts of the Parole Board in your favor."

"Well," I said, "then I sure do appreciate this."

While praying the next night I was given a peace about joining in on this fast, although unlike Dewella, I was going to drink juices. By now I had realized that she was a much stronger

Christian than I, and it would definitely take the grace of God for a person to be able to fast that long without eating anything!

One Saturday morning Rich came by and picked me up. Noticing we were headed in the opposite direction from the beach, I said, "Where we going?"

"Right here, Brother," he nodded as we pulled into the parking lot of a sporting goods store. "Brother Bob has told me you're pretty good on the handball court," said Rich, "so I thought it was about time you took me on in a game of racquetball."

Walking inside, I exclaimed, "But I've never played racquetball."

"Good," he laughed, "then maybe I'll win! Here we are, pick you out a nice racquet and, hmmm, let's see, you're gonna need some gloves, and a sweat band."

"Boy, this is too much," I exclaimed.

Two hours later we were driving home, rather, back to the correctional center.

"Not bad," said Rich. "I only beat you four out of five games!"

"Just you wait until next time," I shouted.

As he pulled into the Center, Rich said, "Oh, by the way, the Lord has put it on my heart to go up to Tallahassee and speak on your behalf at the parole hearing. And, I've talked to Jim Kizer down at Community Release. He's going with me."

Once again I found it very difficult to keep from crying. "This is too much," I stammered. "Why in the world does God keep blessing me so much? All these wonderful people!"

"Because He loves you, Philip," said Rich, "and He won't keep any good thing from those whom He loves."

"I sure wish I could be at the hearing with you," I said.

"Sometimes God sends another to speak for you," replied Rich. "But you'll be there in spirit. You just keep praying and praising, for that's where the victory is won!" added Rich.

✝ ✝ ✝

On June 14, 1983, Dewella broke her fast early. While talking with her over the telephone, she said, "When I was praying for you, the Bible verse which says, 'It is finished' kept coming into my spirit, over and over again. You have the victory, Philip, but only because you got serious and were diligent. And now, once again, a captive is going to be set free!"

✞ ✞ ✞

The next afternoon my name was paged over the loud speaker system again. It was Rich Moore. He was calling from Tallahassee where he'd just attended my hearing.

"Well, Brother, what happened?" I excitedly asked.

"When Commissioner Crockett called your case, he said the panel had voted to confirm the 1985 release date as recommended by Miss Alexander," said Rich.

When he said this my stomach sank. *Two more years*, I thought. "However," paused Rich, "then Jim spoke on your behalf. Afterwards, I said a few words, and Brother, you should have seen the expression on the faces of those three commissioners. Before they looked so proud and certain of their decision. But it looked like something strange began to slowly come over them, and they appeared really humble. As soon as I quit speaking, they huddled and began to whisper."

"What happened?" I demanded.

"Well, when they finally finished," continued Rich, "Commissioner Crockett almost apologetically said, 'The very earliest we can let him out is in August ... 1983.'"

"What???" I shouted. "Did you say '83? That's only two months away! Praise the Lord! P-r-a-i-s-e-e-e-e the L-o-r-d!!!" I sang out.

On August 23, 1983, I was paroled from the Florida prison system.

Six months later I was back at Raiford. This time, Chaplain Shook met me at the front gate. They didn't even shake me down. "He's our guest speaker tonight," Chaplain Shook proudly told the guard.

"Hey, wait a minute," said the sergeant, "this can't be! Ain't this the same Hicks who was assigned to the Motor Pool? Why, he had a Life-plus!"

"Yep, he's the same Hicks," shouted Brother Shook.

✝ ✝ ✝

All Souls Chapel was overflowing that night, and so was my heart. It was filled with love and respect for a lot of men who were there. But I no longer saw them as prisoners. They were my brothers in Christ, and many of them were already free! No longer were they afraid to stand up and be counted for Christ; even in Satan's playground.

As I often did while sharing this miracle testimony, I ended the message by saying, "Would you like to know what God used to set me free?"

"Yes!"

"Amen!"

"Tell us!"

They were the usual shouts.

"I'll tell you what," I paused, "I'll let you know that the next time I speak."

"No-o-o-o-o-o!"

"Tell us now!"

"C'mon, preach it!"

"Well, all right," I said, smiling. "Remember back when I chose to quit compromising, and for the first time in my life I chose to obey God rather than man by telling the whole truth at my trial, instead of half-stepping like I'd done for twenty-nine years—even though my well-meaning public defender warned me against saying a word? Well, when I told the truth as far as the trial judge and prosecutor were concerned, it was all over. After all, I had given a recorded confession the night I got busted. Then, the guy who shot me testified against me. I mean, in the natural everything was stacked against me. Can't say that I blamed their attitudes. But at this point, the judge made a very big mistake. Since he thought it was cut and dried, he stopped the trial and sent the jury in to deliberate. Even my P.D. asked him to read jury instructions, but the judge probably thought, 'Why bother?'

"Well," I continued, "one year later the Supreme Court ruled that as a reversible error, basing their decision on somebody else's case, and my appeal had just hit their desks about the same time. Thus, they had to vacate my entire sentence, and you already know the rest!

"Since I told you how the mistake was made based on the natural so to speak, if you can catch this, it'll bless you outta' your socks!

"The Bible says that God uses 'the foolishness of the world to confound the wise.'[39] And let's face it, in the natural, it probably looked pretty stupid, pretty foolish, for me to come right out and admit guilt!

"But, I now know who really is in control! For God used the foolishness of my admitting my guilt to confound the wise judge, and he made an error! So check this out! If I hadn't been obedient and told the truth, most likely I'd still be doin' time!"

The year following my miracle release, the Florida Supreme Court changed the law back! In essence, God opened the Red Sea to set still another captive free, and the following year God closed the Red Sea again!

When we become Christians, we have to first come to the Cross. We have to be honest about our sinful conditions and admit we need help. We have to face the Cross vertically first, and it's just us and God talkin'. But then afterwards, as Christians, we have to continue in honesty, in a horizontal direction, as we're truthful to those around us. Yes, sometimes it hurts when we have to come right out and admit to things that we'd ordinarily keep to ourselves; activities we'd prefer remain secret.

In fact, even after being set free from a prison constructed of concrete and steel, invisible prisons built out of pride, suppressed anger, denial, and shame continued to keep me held in bondage for years to come and contributed to the embarrassing failure of my first marriage.

Remarried in 1992, my precious wife, Patti, subsequently confronted me about my issues with lust, but I rationalized and justified them as part of human nature. During this time, we joined a local church called the Rock of Roseville, located in northern California. Because of the transparency of our senior pastor, Francis Anfuso, who routinely admitted his own failures in life, I found it so much easier to also come clean. The same desire for truth that I experienced in prison gripped me, and I suddenly found a grace to openly confess my hidden sins. This led to counseling and prayer, and today I walk in freedom!

He whom the Son sets free is free indeed![40]

We're reminded in Scripture that "the king's heart is in the hand of the Lord; Like a river of water, He turns it whithersoever He wills."[41]

I discovered firsthand that it doesn't matter what the judge or parole board says, it is God alone who has the power to "turn hearts" according to His divine design and purpose.

So I encourage you today, right where you are to stop and invite Jesus into your heart. Make Him your personal Savior Lord and fully surrender everything to Him. You'll discover new mercy and grace every morning, and new strength to face today and tomorrow ... regardless of the challenges that will surely come your way.✞

GLOSSARY

B & E – Breaking and Entering

Blues – Prison clothes

Bong – A tall pipe filled with water that is used to smoke cannabis (marijuana) or hashish

Buck – Prison slang for homemade whiskey

Colombian Gold – A premium blend of cannabis (marijuana)

Coke – Cocaine

Cut – Share of the money

Death Row – Where men and women are housed when sentenced to die for specific crimes

Dope – Drugs

Gain time – Time off from a prison sentence because of good behavior or consistent good work within the prison

Girl – Name given to a homosexual in prison, usually who's become so against his will

Hack – A guard

Jailhouse Religion – A term used to describe people who turn to God when in trouble but most often forget about God once he or she is out of trouble

The Joint – Prison

Life plus a dime and a nickel, running wild – A life sentence plus ten years plus five years

A Life Sentence – run consecutively
Misdemeanor – A crime that is less serious than a felony but more serious than an infraction
Ol' slewfoot – A name for Satan or the devil
P.D. – Public Defender
Pair of fives – Two five-year prison sentences
Prayed-Up – An old term for maintaining a daily discipline of prayer
Road Kill – An animal or bird that has been run over by a vehicle
Shank – A homemade knife or weapon
Short-Timer – An inmate who has a short time to go before being released
Sissy – Homosexual
Snitch – To tell on someone, usually to gain favor
Snow – Cocaine
S.O.S. – An acronym for "same old stuff." A four-letter word that means human waste
Stinger – A device constructed of Popsicle sticks, razor blades, rubber bands, and wire that is used to heat water for coffee
Stripes – Refers to the beating Jesus endured before His crucifixion; specifically, stripes are bloody whip marks on His body
Swapping hands – Fighting
Trusty – A title given to an inmate who requires minimum security, one who is "trusted" by authorities and is allowed outside his or her cell to perform various duties
Turkish Hash – A much stronger form of cannabis (marijuana) that originates in the country of Turkey
Yellow – Scared or afraid

SOME FINAL COMMENTS

Between 1993 and 1999, my wife Patti and I lived in southern California, where we were members of Church on the Way (COTW). We served in children's ministry, outreach, and other areas, and also attended a "Young Marrieds Group" pastored by Scott and Becky Bauer, who later became the senior ministers of COTW.

The son-in-law of Pastor Jack Hayford, Scott took me aside one evening and encouraged me with these words: "Philip, don't you feel you're called to children's evangelism?"

I quickly responded to this wonderful man of God by saying, "Oh, no. I'm called to prison ministry! I've got this amazing testimony, and I've ministered in places like San Quentin, Lancaster, and the prison in Tijuana, Mexico!"

By no coincidence (there are none with God!), shortly after my prideful response to Scott's encouragement, the door slammed shut on prison ministry and opened WIDE to children's ministry!

We began ministering to children in churches, schools, and outreaches all over California, and folks began to call me "the pig man," as I had created and personified a country character known as "Cuz'n Philburt & Wilburt the Pot-Belly-Pig!"

God brought us to northern California in 1999, and we subsequently incorporated as A Merry Heart Ministries. I was so very honored when I was later ordained by Pastor Francis Anfuso at the Rock of Roseville, California, and even more doors opened to minister God's love and laughter to His children and their families.

Throughout this time I began dying to self more and more while simultaneously admitting I needed more help with hooks of anger and lust that had held me captive for years. This led to further counseling and accountability, and today I am FREE!

Now walking in more wholeness and integrity than ever before, the Spirit of the Lord is now upon me as never before—to passionately minister in prisons, churches, and especially at men's meetings—encouraging all to lay aside their reputations and come clean off the hooks that are holding them captive!

We covet your prayerful support of A Merry Heart Ministries (www.amerryheart.com). Your purchase of this book will help fund the calling upon our lives to preach freedom to the captives—whether they are in a prison cell or sitting far too comfortably in a church pew!

While God has surely proven Himself faithful to miraculously set me free from a prison constructed of concrete and steel, I have since made many bad choices. My next book will describe the circumstances and forces that caused my disobedience but, most importantly, it will also describe the steps I had to take to be completely restored and taken to a new depth with Jesus—steps that set my feet to dancing and gave me a new song that others now hear and desire for their lives!

END NOTES

[1] "For I do not understand my own actions—I am baffled, bewildered. I do not practice or accomplish what I wish, but I do the very thing that I loathe or what my moral instinct condemns" (Romans 7:15).

[2] "For it is by free grace (God's unmerited favor) that you are saved (delivered from eternal judgment and made partakers of Christ's salvation) through your faith. And his salvation is not of yourselves, or of your own doing. It is a free gift, not of works lest any man should boast. It is not the result of what any one can possibly do, so no one can pride himself in it or take glory to himself" (Ephesians 2:8-9).

[3] "And this is the testimony, record or promise: God gave us eternal life, and this life is in His Son. He who has the Son has (eternal) life; he who does not have the Son of God does not have that life" (1 John 5:11-12).

[4] "My God will liberally supply your every need according to His riches in glory in Christ Jesus" (Philippians 4:19).

[5] *Joni*. Written by Joe Musser and Joni Eareckson Tada. Published by Zondervan August 2001 (25th Anniversary edition).

[6] "Do all things without grumbling and complaining (against God), that you may show yourselves to be blameless and harmless, children of God in the midst of a crooked and perverse generation, among whom you are seen as bright lights" (Philippians 2:14-15).

[7] Jesus said, "But I tell you, Love your enemies and pray for those who persecute you. To show that you are children of your Father

who is in heaven, for He makes His sun rise on the wicked and on the good, and makes the rain fall upon the upright and the wrongdoers (alike). For if you love those who love you, what reward can you have? Do not even the tax collectors do that?" (Matthew 5:44-46)

[8] "I planted, Apollos watered, but God was making it grow, and He gave the increase" (1 Corinthians 3:6).

[9] "For all who are led by the Spirit of God are sons of God" (Romans 8:14).

[10] "Beloved, never avenge yourselves, but leave the way open for [God's] wrath; for it is written, Vengeance is Mine, I will repay, says the Lord" (Romans 12:19).

[11] "Do not be deceived and misled: God will not allow Himself to be sneered at or mocked. He deludes himself who attempts to delude God. For whatever a man sows, that and that only is what he will reap" (Galatians 6:7).

[12] "Train up a child in the way he should go and when he is old he will not depart from it" (Proverbs 22:6).

[13] "And God said, Behold, I have given you every herb bearing seed, which is upon the face of all the earth, and every tree whose fruit yields seed; to you it shall be for food" (Genesis 1:29).

[14] "For your heavenly Father knows that you need all these things" (Matthew 6:32).

[15] "My God will liberally supply (fill to the full) your every need according to His riches in glory in Christ Jesus" (Philippians 4:19).

[16] "Not that I am implying that I was in any personal want, for I have learned how to be content (satisfied to the point where I am not disturbed or disquieted) in whatever state I am" (Philippians 4:11).

[17] "Look at the birds of the air; they neither sow nor reap nor gather into barns, and yet your heavenly Father keeps feeding them. Are you not worth more than they?" (Matthew 6:26)

[18] "Do not fret or have anxiety about anything, but in every circumstance and in everything by prayer and petition (definite requests) with thanksgiving continue to make your wants known to God" (Philippians 4:6).

[19] "There hath no temptation taken you but such as is common to man; but God is faithful, who will not suffer (allow) you to be tempted above (more than) that ye are able; but will with the temptation also make a way to escape, that ye may be able to bear it" (1 Corinthians 10:13).

[20] "Do not be deceived and misled: God will not allow Himself to be sneered at or mocked. For whatever a man sows, that and that only is what he will reap" (Galatians 6:7).

[21] "Blessed (happy) is the man, who walks not in the counsel of the ungodly, Nor stands in the path of sinners, Nor sits in the seat of the scornful" (Psalms 1:1).

[22] "Trust in the Lord with all thine heart and lean not to your own understanding. In ALL things acknowledge Him and He will direct your paths" (Proverbs 3:5-6).

[23] "Little children, you are of God—you belong to Him—and have [already] defeated and overcome them [the agents of antichrist], because He Who lives in you is greater (mightier) than he who is in the world" (1 John 4:4).

[24] "So then Pilate took Jesus and scourged (whipped) Him. And the soldiers, having twisted a crown of thorns, put it on His head..." (John 19:2a)

[25] Matthew 10:28 assures us, "And do not be afraid of those who kill the body but cannot kill the soul, but rather be afraid of him who can destroy both soul and body in hell."

[26] "I have been crucified with Christ (in Him)—I have shared His crucifixion; it is no longer I who live, but Christ, the Messiah, lives in me; and the life I now live in the body I live by faith—reliance on and complete trust—in the Son of God, Who loved me and gave Himself up for me" (Galatians 2:20).

[27] "When a man's ways please the Lord, He makes even his enemies to be at peace with him" (Proverbs 16:7).

[28] "As you therefore have received Christ Jesus the Lord, so walk in Him, rooted and built up in Him and established in the faith, as you have been taught, abounding in it with thanksgiving" (Colossians 2:6-7).

[29] "Thank God in everything—no matter what the circumstances may

be, be thankful and give thanks; for this is the will of God for you (who are) in Christ Jesus" (1 Thessalonians 5:18).

[30] Jesus said, "With men this is impossible, but all things are possible with God" (Matthew 19:26).

[31] "To console those who mourn in Zion. To give them beauty for ashes, the oil of joy for mourning, The garment of praise for the spirit of heaviness" (Isaiah 61:3).

[32] "But without faith it is impossible to please and be satisfactory to Him. For whoever would come near to God must believe that God exists and that He is a Rewarder of those who earnestly and diligently seek Him" (Hebrews 11:6).

[33] "When you pass through the waters, I will be with you; And through the rivers, they shall not overflow you. When you walk through the fire, you shall not be burned, Nor shall the flame scorch you" (Isaiah 43:2).

[34] Matthew 13:24-30 and 36-43 provide a clear parable of the tares among the wheat.

[35] "And I will give you the keys of the kingdom of heaven, and whatever you bind on earth will be bound in heaven, and whatever you loose on earth will be loosed in heaven" (Matthew 16:19).

[36] In Ephesians 6:18, after "putting on the whole armor of God" we're instructed to "Pray at all times—on every occasion, in every season—in the Spirit, with all [manner of] prayer and entreaty."

[37] "Jesus Christ, the same yesterday, today and forever!" (Hebrews 13:8)

[38] "Praising God, and having favour and goodwill with all the people" (Acts 2:47).

[39] "God selected—deliberately chose—what in the world is foolish to put the wise to shame, and what the world calls weak to put the strong to shame" (1 Corinthians 1:27).

[40] "Whom the Son sets free is free indeed" (John 8:36).

[41] "The King's (man's) heart is in the hand of the Lord; like a river of living water, He (God) turns it whatsoever He wills" (Proverbs 21:3).

ABOUT THE AUTHOR

Philip Hicks was ordained as an Evangelist in 2001 by Pastor Francis Anfuso at the Rock of Roseville, California. The founder of A Merry Heart Ministries, Philip routinely ministers in prisons and churches and performs "entertainment with a message" in public schools throughout the state of California.

In addition, he and his performing pig minister coast to coast, and Philip's wife Patti performs as "Patticakes the Klown," bringing the joy of our Lord to many!

Philip was recently named West Coast Director of Evangelism Explosion's International Prison Ministry.

Philip, Patti and Cody Hicks now make their home in northern California. Indeed, life is NEVER a "boar" at their home! Or is it?